Regionalism and Security Challenges in South and Central Asia

Navigating Geopolitical Shifts

Regionalism and Security Challenges in South and Central Asia

Navigating Geopolitical Shifts

Edited by

Nivedita Das Kundu

PENTAGON PRESS LLP

First published in 2025 by
PENTAGON PRESS LLP
206, Peacock Lane, Shahpur Jat
New Delhi-110049, India
Contact: 011-26490600

Typeset in Times New Roman, 12 Point
Printed at Aegean Offset Printers, Greater Noida

ISBN 978-81-991162-2-1

Disclaimer: *The views and opinions expressed in the book are the individual assertion of the Authors. The Publisher does not take any responsibility for the same in any manner whatsoever. The same shall solely be the responsibility of the Authors.*

www.pentagonpress.in

This book is dedicated to students of
International Relations and Diplomacy

Contents

Preface

This book's chapters examine the evolving discourse on regionalism within one of the most strategically important regions of the contemporary world. South and Central Asia have historically functioned as a crossroads of civilizations, facilitating cultural exchange, trade, and political interaction along the ancient Silk Road. In the present era, this historical legacy converges with new geopolitical dynamics, positioning the region once again at the center of global attention.

This study conceptualizes regionalism through two principal discourses: integration and connectivity. The integration discourse emphasizes the creation of cohesive frameworks for security cooperation, economic partnership, and cultural interaction among the regional states. Whereas the connectivity discourse highlights infrastructure development and trade linkages that transcend national borders, reinforcing the region's role as a hub of intercontinental exchange. Both discourses underscore the opportunities and complexities inherent in fostering regional cooperation.

Security challenges remain a central concern for the whole region. The region's geographical proximity to Afghanistan, coupled with the activities of extremist groups, has heightened vulnerabilities. Porous borders, inter-ethnic tensions, and unresolved historical disputes compound these challenges. Regional organizations have sought to address these issues through multilateral security frameworks, yet the outcomes remain uneven and contested.

The chapters in this book employ a mixed-methods approach, combining historical and content analysis with expert views and opinions and case studies of regional projects and initiatives.

The content in this book provides both depth and breadth in examining the intersection of historical legacies, contemporary policies, and prospects for regionalism in Central Asia.

Ultimately, this book argues that regionalism in Central Asia is a dynamic and evolving process. While it offers considerable potential for promoting economic growth, cultural revival, and political stability, it remains profoundly shaped by the shifting geopolitical strategies of global powers and the region's internal complexities. The chapters in this book will provide broader theoretical and comparative debates on regionalism, this study seeks to contribute to the academic literature on regional cooperation, security, and connectivity in the twenty-first century.

Nivedita Das Kundu

Acknowledgements

The creation of this Book, "Regionalism and Security Challenges in South and Central Asia: Navigating Geopolitical Shifts," emerged from a dedicated effort to foster deeper insights into the subject under study. The formation of this book owes itself to the unwavering encouragement extended by academics, scholars, strategic analysts, foreign policy experts, practitioners, and policymakers. Their valuable insights and contributions have illuminated various pertinent topics, forming the cornerstone of this endeavour.

A debt of gratitude is owed to my colleagues and friends within the strategic and academic community for their invaluable support. Their tireless dedication and contributions amidst their busy schedules have been instrumental in shaping this compiled volume. Without their steadfast support, this undertaking would not have come into existence. Special mention goes to Professor Bakhodir Mamurov, Rector, Bukhara State Pedagogical Institute, Professor Sherzod Muradov, Vice Rector, Bukhara State Pedagogical Institute, Professor Alisher Nazarov from University of Management and Future Technologies, and Professor Sanjar Kurbanov, Bukhara State Pedagogical Institute, their support has been truly exceptional for the outcome of this book.

A heartfelt acknowledgment is extended to all the contributors, whose collaborative spirit and willingness to share their profound knowledge have enriched this work. Their insightful and thought-provoking ideas have infused this Book with depth and significance.

I am also indebted to my family members, whose unwavering support and cooperative attitude have been a pillar of strength throughout this research project's execution and the subsequent completion of this edited volume. Their contribution cannot be adequately expressed in words, and their support has been invaluable.

Furthermore, I extend my gratitude to the administrative and academic teams, students, and volunteers of the Uzbekistan State World Languages University, Bukhara State Pedagogical Institute, and to Bharat Centre of Canada research team; their encouragement and cooperation have played a pivotal role in this endeavour. I would also like to thank the libraries of Uzbekistan State World Languages University, United Services Institution of India's library, Brampton-City Library, and York University's Library for their unwavering support, even though space constraints prevent me from acknowledging them individually. Their contributions have been highly appreciated.

In its current form, this volume stands as a testament to the whole-hearted collaboration and assistance of all the contributors. It is my sincere hope that readers, students of international relations, foreign policy analysts, and policymakers will find value in the chapters of the book on "Regionalism and Security Challenges in South and Central Asia: Navigating Geopolitical Shifts."

Nivedita Das Kundu

Contributors' Profiles

Professor Sharaf Agabayev (PHD, DSC Candidate)
Professor, Department of Political Science, Uzbekistan State World Languages University, Tashkent, Uzbekistan

Maj. Gen. Shashi Bhushan Asthana (Retd., PhD)
Veteran Infantry General with extensive national and international experience; Chief Instructor, United Services Institute of India; Advisor and Professor, Amity International University, Noida; Advisor, Foreign Policy Institute; Advisor, Global Consultants Corporation, India

Professor Erkin Baidarov (PhD)
Professor, Institute of Oriental Studies, Almaty, Kazakhstan

Dr. Dinara Dauyen (PhD)
Researcher, Institute of Oriental Studies, Almaty, Kazakhstan

Professor Nivedita Das Kundu (PhD, DSC Candidate)
Professor, Department of Political Science and International Relations, Uzbekistan State World Languages University, Tashkent; Affiliated Professor, York University, Toronto, Canada

Maj. Gen. Jagatbir Singh (Retd.)
Distinguished Fellow, United Services Institute of India; Professor, Shiv Nadar University, Noida, India

Professor Anvar Kadirov (DSC)
Professor, Department of Political Science and Philosophy, Al-Farghanus University, Tashkent, Uzbekistan

Dr. Kulaisha Nazarova (PhD)
Researcher, Institute of Oriental Studies, Almaty, Kazakhstan

Ms. Shakhrozoda Anvarovna (PhD Candidate)
Lecturer, Department of Political Science, Uzbekistan State World Languages University, Tashkent, Uzbekistan

Professor Nazgul Radzhapova (PhD)
Professor, International Department, Osh State University, Osh, Kyrgyzstan

Professor Sanjar Saidov (DSC)
Professor of International Relations and Political Science, Uzbekistan State World Languages University, Tashkent, Uzbekistan

Dr. Hamroyev Saidjon Sanoyevich (PhD)
Associate Professor, Department of Social Sciences, BuxDPI, Uzbekistan

Professor Alina Tashybayeva (PhD)
Professor, Department of English, Osh State University, Osh, Kyrgyzstan

Ms. Aygerim Temirbaeva (PhD Candidate)
Lecturer, Department of Political Science, Uzbekistan State World Languages University, Tashkent, Uzbekistan

Mr. Omonboy Khaytimmatov (PhD Candidate)
Lecturer, Department of Political Science, Uzbekistan State World Languages University, Tashkent, Uzbekistan

Professor Zakir Usmanov (PhD)
Associate Professor, Department of Oil and Gas Economics, Russian State University of Oil and Gas, Tashkent, Uzbekistan

Professor Zokir Zamonov (PhD, DSC Candidate)
Professor, Department of Social Sciences, Uzbekistan State World Languages University, Tashkent, Uzbekistan

Dr. Uzakbaev (PhD)
Researcher, Institute of Oriental Studies, Almaty, Kazakhstan

Professor Movkebaeva G.I. Uzakbaev (PhD)
Professor, Institute of Oriental Studies, Almaty, Kazakhstan

Ms. Altynay Mambetova (PhD Candidate)
Lecturer, Department of International Relations, Kenzhegali Sagadiyev University of International Business, Almaty, Kazakhstan

List of Abbreviation

ADB	Asian Development Bank
AI	Artificial Intelligence
AIIB	Asian Infrastructure Investment Bank
BIMSTEC	Bay of Bengal Initiative for Multi-Sectoral Technical and Economic Cooperation
BRI	Belt and Road Initiative
BRICS	Brazil, Russia, India, China, and South Africa
BTWC	Biological and Toxin Weapons Convention
C5+1	Cooperation Format between the 5 Central Asian States and the United States
CAC	Central Asian Cooperation
CACO	Central Asian Cooperation Organization
CAEC	Central Asian Economic Community
CAPS	Central Asian Power System
CAU	Central Asian Union
CAREC	Regional Environmental Center for Central Asia
CASA-1000	Central Asia–South Asia Electricity Transmission and Trade Project
C+C5	China–Central Asia Format
CICA	Conference on Interaction and Confidence-Building Measures in Asia
CIS	Commonwealth of Independent States

CIS FTA	Commonwealth of Independent States Free Trade Agreement
CKU	China–Kyrgyzstan–Uzbekistan (Railway)
CO_2	Carbon Dioxide
CPEC	China–Pakistan Economic Corridor
CSTO	Collective Security Treaty Organization
CWC	Chemical Weapons Convention
EAEU	Eurasian Economic Union
ECO	Economic Cooperation Organization
EU	European Union
FAO	Food and Agriculture Organization (of the United Nations)
G20	Group of Twenty
GDP	Gross Domestic Product
GEF	Global Environment Facility
GSI	Global Security Initiative
IAEA	International Atomic Energy Agency
ICWC	Interstate Commission for Water Coordination
IEA	International Energy Agency
INSTC	International North–South Transport Corridor
IOR	Indian Ocean Region
IOR-ARC	Indian Ocean Rim Association for Regional Cooperation
IORA	Indian Ocean Rim Association
IPCC	Intergovernmental Panel on Climate Change
IUCN	International Union for Conservation of Nature
IWRM	Integrated Water Resources Management
km^3	Cubic kilometre
kWh	Kilowatt-hour

MW	Megawatt
NATO	North Atlantic Treaty Organization
NGO(s)	Non-Governmental Organization(s)
NOC	National Oil Companies
OIC	Organization of Islamic Cooperation
Oliy Majlis	Supreme Assembly (Parliament of Uzbekistan)
OPEC	Organization of the Petroleum Exporting Countries
OSCE	Organization for Security and Co-operation in Europe
PPP(s)	Public–Private Partnership(s)
PR	Public Relations
RATS	Regional Anti-Terrorist Structure
RES	Renewable Energy Sources
SAARC	South Asian Association for Regional Cooperation
SCO	Shanghai Cooperation Organization
SO_2 –	Sulfur Dioxide
SREB	Silk Road Economic Belt
SWOT	Strengths, Weaknesses, Opportunities, and Threats
TAPI	Turkmenistan–Afghanistan–Pakistan–India (Gas Pipeline)
TASIM	Trans-Eurasian Information Super Highway
TRACECA	Transport Corridor Europe–Caucasus–Asia
TUTAP	Turkmenistan–Uzbekistan–Tajikistan–Afghanistan–Pakistan (Power Project)
U.S. / US	United States
UN	United Nations
UNDP	United Nations Development Programme
UNECE	United Nations Economic Commission for Europe
UNEP	United Nations Environment Programme

UNESCO	United Nations Educational, Scientific and Cultural Organization
UNSC	United Nations Security Council
USSR	Union of Soviet Socialist Republics
VUCA	Volatility, Uncertainty, Complexity, and Ambiguity
WHO	World Health Organization
WMO	World Meteorological Organization
WTO	World Trade Organization
WWF	World Wide Fund for Nature
USD	United States Dollar

Introduction

Nivedita Das Kundu

The edited volume, "Regionalism and Security Challenges in South and Central Asia: Navigating Geopolitical Shifts", examines the profound transformations occurring across South and Central Asia as a result of shifting global power dynamics, economic realignments, and emerging security threats. In recent years, these regions have found themselves at the epicentre of complex geopolitical processes influenced by both traditional rivalries and evolving multilateral partnerships. The active engagement of major powers such as China, Russia, and India, alongside the growing institutional influence of various regional organizations, has reshaped the regional security architecture.

This edited volume explores how traditional and non-traditional security threats, including terrorism, cyber threats, environmental degradation, and energy insecurity, have complicated the stability of the region. At a time when regionalism is being redefined by infrastructure projects, political consultations, and collaborative security initiatives, this volume brings together the writings from a diverse group of scholars, practitioners, and policymakers to offer critical perspectives on the evolving trends.

This book is divided into three thematic sections. All the chapters provides an analytical foundation to understand changing political landscape and the regional strategies of key actors. The chapters discusses the Security Challenges, it delves into both internal and cross-border security issues faced by South and Central Asian states, particularly focusing on evolving security doctrines and strategic responses. The chapters also discusses about the geopolitical shifts and regionalism process in Central Asia. Some chapters highlighted the growing significance of Central Asia as a geostrategic hub, discussing national interests, regional cooperation efforts, and the viability of a Central Asian Union formation. Chapters also discusses about the regional cooperation mechanisms & multilateral approaches. Chapters also discusses about the role of regional institutions, as well as broader multilateral frameworks, in addressing security and integration challenges.

The chapters in this volume address a broad spectrum of issues, from silk route connectivity and strategic partnerships to environmental security, energy corridors, and multilateral diplomacy. With case studies from across the region, including India, Uzbekistan, Kazakhstan, and Kyrgyzstan, the book provides a nuanced understanding of regional cooperation in the face of global uncertainty. For example, the chapter on "Interaction Between Kazakhstan and China within the Framework of Regionalism Policy in Asia," explores Kazakhstan's strategic engagement with China in the context of regional integration. It highlights Kazakhstan's multi-vector foreign policy and China's influence through initiatives such as the "Central Asia-China" (C5+1) dialogue, SCO, and CICA. The chapter explained China as a "corridor of opportunities", in Kazakhstan's regionalist vision. Another chapter on "Regional Transport Networks: Silk Route Regionalism and Connectivity Expansion," focused on infrastructure-led integration. This Chapter explained the concept of silk route regionalism. One of the chapters also analyzed investment opportunities in the transport network sectors, such as roads, railways, and logistics hubs, and their role in restoring historical trade corridors, lowering customs barriers, and enhancing the regional economy. Another chapter on "Environmental Security in Central Asia", addresses major environmental issues in Central Asia, including the Aral Sea crisis, desertification, and water scarcity. Using political, geographic, and economic perspectives, it presents three future scenarios shaped by regional cooperation, mismanagement, and climate change. The chapter on "National Interests of Uzbekistan in the Context of the New Geopolitical Order", analysed Uzbekistan's strategic position and national development goals, which are examined against the backdrop of a multipolar world. The chapter emphasizes balancing sovereignty and foreign influence while leveraging country's geographic and resource advantages for regional stability. The Chapter on "Dynamics of Strategic Partnership Between Central Asian States", analyzed the period 2017–2024. The chapter outlines evolving strategic partnerships in Central Asia aimed at addressing environmental, energy, and political issues. It highlights the significance of regional consultative meetings among heads of state. The chapter on the "Possibility of the Formation of the Central Asian Union: Impact on Regionalism," this Chapter discusses the prospects for a Central Asian Union. It identified common challenges and shared history as grounds for cooperation but emphasizes the critical role of political commitment, regional consensus, and strategic alignment. The chapter on "The Principle of Justice in Central Asian Reforms: A Guarantee of Peace and Security," mentioned that justice is positioned as a foundation for long-term peace. This shapter examines Uzbekistan's reform agenda and its relevance for reducing inequality, enhancing civic participation, and promoting inclusive development in a competitive geopolitical environment. The chapter on the "Process of Regionalism in Central Asia", applying regionalism theory, examines political, economic, and environmental integration in Central Asia. It reviews institutional mechanisms and challenges such as trade harmonization and political fragmentation, proposing cooperative models for regional stability. The Chapter on the topic of "Security Challenges for India in South Asia", explained the scope of India's security concerns to include cyber threats, environmental hazards, and economic vulnerabilities. This Chapter recommends a comprehensive and adaptive security policy to navigate internal and external risks. The chapter on "Strategic Focus and Role of China in the SCO", explained the use of a SWOT framework, that evaluates China's growing role in the SCO, focusing on its economic diplomacy and strategic policymaking. Recommendations were given in the Chapter for enhancing the organization's influence under changing global dynamics.

The chapter on "Strengthening Military and Security Cooperation in the SCO: An Indian Perspective", reviews India's engagement in the SCO military and security frameworks. In this chapter emphasis is placed on counter-terrorism, cyber threats, and defense collaboration, along with the strategic and institutional constraints that India faces. The chapter on "SCO and the Changed Regional

Security Architecture", this chapter investigated how SCO's enlargement, particularly under Kazakhstan's leadership, affects its ability to address terrorism, separatism, and new regional threats. It also explores the structural adaptations needed for effective governance. The chapter on "The Role of the SCO in Shaping Regional Security Dynamics in Central Asia", in this chapter, a comparative study of SCO's security role versus other regional organizations is presented. It outlines internal limitations and future opportunities, stressing the need for reforms and institutional strengthening options to enhance regional peace and security. The chapter on "Decoding Geopolitical Shift and South Asia: How Can India Navigate Its Security Interests"? mentioned India's strategic posture in a shifting global environment. Key themes include the rise of cyber warfare, climate security, and India's approach to global alliances and indigenous defense innovation. The chapter on the "Role of Regional and International Organizations in Kyrgyzstan's Foreign Policy", explores Kyrgyzstan's multilateral diplomacy through organizations like the SCO, UN, and CIS. It focuses on Kyrgyzstan's regional goals, infrastructure initiatives, and role in shaping collective development agendas. The Chapter on the "Fundamental and Applied Problems of Integration of Central Asian Countries," dealt with the structural obstacles to Central Asian integration, including political fragmentation and infrastructure gaps. It offers tailored solutions emphasizing different cooperation strategies in transport and energy.

This volume is both timely and relevant, offering well-documented analyses grounded in empirical evidence and policy insight. The chapters in this volume is expected to serve as a valuable resource for scholars, strategic analysts, policymakers, and students of international relations. Furthermore, the diverse perspectives and region-specific studies included in the book contribute to a more comprehensive understanding of the dynamics shaping South and Central Asia today.

SECTION I

Geopolitical Shifts and Regionalism in Central Asia

1

Geopolitical Shifts and Regionalism in Central Asia

Anvar Kadirov

ABSTRACT

In his famous Fulton speech in 1946, delivered after the Second World War, Sir Winston Churchill, one of the patriarchs of political science, defining the direction of British foreign policy, sarcastically emphasized that "Britain has no permanent friends or permanent enemies, but permanent interests." This statement remains equally relevant today: within the global geopolitical landscape, all significant political actors in the contemporary "political game," continue to advance their national geopolitical interests.

With the collapse of the bipolar world order at the end of the twentieth century and the conclusion of the Cold War, the tendency towards the formation of a multipolar political order has emerged. However, this tendency has not removed but rather aggravated the difficulties associated with realizing national interests, particularly for young and developing states.

Located at the very heart of Central Asia, and aptly described by the English political scientist Halford Mackinder as the "Heartland," Uzbekistan is no exception. Its geopolitical position, geostrategic significance, and population of 37 million (with an annual growth of over 1 million), combined with stable economic development and abundant natural resources, make Uzbekistan attractive to the geopolitical interests of leading international powers. The country serves as a focal point for the national interests of China, Russia, the United States, developed Asia-Pacific countries such as South Korea and Japan, as well as, European states and the European Union.

In this context, safeguarding the national interests of independent Uzbekistan, ensuring sovereignty, political independence, and sustainable socio-economic development has become critically important. This chapter highlights Uzbekistan's national interests within the broader framework of the evolving architecture of the global political order.

Keywords: *Geopolitics, national interests, world order, sovereignty, national independence, security, stability.*

The year 1991 was a pivotal turning point in the transformation of society and statehood in Central Asia, marked by the emergence of five newly independent states, Uzbekistan, Kazakhstan, Turkmenistan, Kyrgyzstan, and Tajikistan, on the global political map. The "Independence Parade," initiated by then-President of Russia Boris Yeltsin, provided significant impetus to the formation of these new sovereign states in the post-Soviet political space. With the attainment of independence, the former Soviet republics of Central Asia embarked upon democratic paths of socio-economic development.

However, the implementation of democratic reforms, particularly in Uzbekistan, has been constrained by the legacy of Soviet political culture. Decades of communist ideology entrenched authoritarian psychology, stifled human rights, and alienated individuals from labor and property. As acknowledged by the First President of Uzbekistan, Islam Karimov, the mentality and psychology shaped under the command-bureaucratic system cannot be instantly eradicated; their transformation requires years of gradual change.

Taking these realities into account, Karimov advanced his well-known concept of the "Uzbek Model" of transformation and modernization, emphasizing gradual, large-scale reforms. The centralization of political power, however, inevitably fostered authoritarian tendencies, political passivity, and a personality cult. The backbone of any market economy, economic freedom and the institution of private property, was severely restricted, if not outright prohibited, under the Soviet regime. Consequently, uneven economic development arose across the Central Asian region, particularly between states that embraced economic liberalization and those that did not.

Kazakhstan provides a notable example: through policies of economic liberalization, foreign investment, and joint ventures, it achieved significant social welfare improvements in a short period. This led to increased labor migration from Uzbekistan to Kazakhstan by the late 1990s. Kazakhstan's approach mirrored that of Deng Xiaoping's reforms in post-Mao China, which prioritized modernization, economic freedom, and private enterprise. In contrast to Europe, however, Central Asian states lacked the historical evolution of private property institutions, capitalist traditions, or reformist movements. Consequently, their trajectory has been comparatively shorter and more constrained.

A major shift occurred with the rise of Uzbekistan's new political leadership in 2017 under President Shavkat Mirziyoyev, who broke with previous models by introducing the "Strategy of accelerated development of Uzbekistan (2017–2021)." This was followed by the "Development Strategy 2022–2026" and plans extending to 2030, aimed at modernizing the economy, creating free trade zones, and promoting joint ventures. While these policies have advanced economic liberalization, they have also heightened vulnerabilities related to financial security, particularly through dependence on foreign investment and dominance of foreign-manufactured goods, notably from China.

At the core of Uzbekistan's national interests lies the economic welfare of its population: alleviating poverty, reducing labor migration, and strengthening sovereignty. The Development Strategy emphasizes reinforcing independence, enhancing Uzbekistan's role in international relations, and fostering an environment of security, stability, and good-neighbourly relations. However, these interests frequently clash with the predatory policies of advanced states, which apply strategies of "soft power." Unlike overt military coercion, soft power is exercised through loans and credits with high interest rates, creating long-term economic dependence. As the saying goes, "Free cheese exists only in a mousetrap."

Scholars have long recognized this dynamic. Turkish analyst I. Kusureli observed in the 1980s that wealthy states providing "aid" always prioritized their own interests. Similarly, German Chancellor Helmut Schmidt warned that developing states, persuaded into liberalizing markets and accepting short-term loans, often fell prey to foreign speculation and crushing debt burdens. Uzbek scholar R. Alimov further cautioned that such "assistance" could destabilize not only Central Asia's socio-economic well-being but also regional and global security, particularly given the region's multi-ethnic and multi-confessional composition.

Indeed, economic levers often prove more effective than military ones. Uzbekistan today represents a geopolitical intersection where the interests of the United States, Russia, and increasingly China converge. China, with its expanding economy and reliance on soft power, has flooded Central Asian markets with consumer goods and aspires to global superpower status, challenging U.S dominance. American political scientist Zbigniew Brzezinski argued that U.S. hegemony was sustained by unrivalled military reach, economic dynamism, technological leadership, and cultural appeal, granting Washington a political influence unmatched by other states.

Currently, Central Asia has become a contested space in the renewed "Great Game" among China, Russia, the United States, and Turkey. Each power seeks dominance over the region, rich in hydrocarbon resources and strategically located yet economically underdeveloped. The geopolitical landscape is shaped by numerous regional organizations such as the SCO, CIS, and Eurasian Economic Community. Uzbekistan, a member of the SCO since 2001, actively engages in initiatives such as the Convention on Combating International Terrorism, Extremism, and Separatism. Nevertheless, the SCO remains dominated by the geopolitical agendas of China and Russia.

China's "One Belt, One Road," initiative, advanced by President Xi Jinping, represents both a revival of East–West civilizational dialogue and a tool for promoting the interests of leading powers. Meanwhile, Russia, motivated by imperial ambitions, continues to exert influence through alliances such as the CSTO and Eurasian Economic Community. The ongoing Russia–Ukraine conflict and shifting balances of power between Russia and the United States are reshaping the architecture of the global order.

In this evolving landscape, Uzbekistan emphasizes equality, mutual respect, and peaceful dispute resolution as guiding principles of its foreign policy. As President Shavkat Mirziyoyev declared at the September 2022 SCO Summit in Samarkand: "The SCO is strong if each of us is strong." This statement underscores Uzbekistan's commitment to pursuing its national interests through sovereignty, stability, good-neighborly relations, and active engagement within the framework of the new global geopolitical architecture.

REFERENCES

Alimov R.M. Central Asia: community of interests, T.: "Shark", 2005.
Central Asia. 120 years of Russian Rule. Ed. by Edward Allworth. Duke University Press. 1989.
Kuchuradi I. Economic inequality, human rights, democracy, and the free market.//Problems of philosophy.-1966, no.
Mirziyoyev Sh. Yangi Uzbekiston Tarakkiyot strategysi.-T.: "Uzbekistan". 2022.
Schmitt G. The burden of global responsibility. A European view of the prospects for universal development. // Russia in global politics-2002. № 2. November-December.
Zbigniew Brzezinski. The Grand Chessboard. M: "International Relations".
Shanghai Cooperation Organization. [Electronic resource] //RIA 2022. September 15.

2

Decoding Geopolitical Shifts in South Asia: India's Strategic Navigation of Security Interests

Shashi Bhushan Asthana

ABSTRACT

South Asia's geopolitical environment is undergoing profound transformation, shaped by global power shifts, regional conflicts, and emerging multidimensional security threats. India, as the largest and most influential actor in the region, faces a wide range of challenges including territorial disputes, terrorism, radicalisation, political instability, technological warfare, and climate change. This chapter examines how India navigates these complexities, balancing its relations with major powers such as the United States, Russia, and China, while strengthening cooperation within regional frameworks including SAARC, BIMSTEC, IORA, and the Shanghai Cooperation Organisation (SCO).

The analysis also situates South Asia within the broader context of renewed great-power rivalry, sometimes referred to as "Cold War 2.0", as well as, cyber threats, outer-space militarisation, and energy security. Particular emphasis is given to India's strategic responses through military modernisation, pragmatic diplomacy, and multilateral partnerships. The chapter concludes that India's unique geopolitical position, sharing borders with two nuclear adversaries in collusion, enquires a calibrated balance of deterrence, regional engagement, and global strategic alignment.

Keywords: *South Asia, India, Geopolitical transformation, Great-power rivalry / Cold War 2.0, Terrorism and radicalisation, Border disputes, Nuclear rivalry, Cybersecurity & technological war, Climate change & environmental insecurity, Strategic autonomy & multilateralism, Military modernisation & Atmanirbhar (self-dependent) Bharat, Regionalism*

> *"India is the only country in the world that has two nuclear neighbours with whom it shares unresolved border disputes, which have already led to wars in the past, and both of them are in strategic collusion with each other."*

Backdrop

The contemporary international order is marked by increasing volatility and uncertainty. Intensifying great-power competition, particularly between the United States and China, is reshaping the strategic environment across Asia. Simultaneously, the war in Ukraine has triggered new alignments and revealed vulnerabilities in global supply chains, energy markets, and multilateral institutions.

South Asia, positioned at the intersection of West Asia, Central Asia, and the Indo-Pacific, is acutely affected by these global dynamics. Regional conflicts, unresolved border disputes, rising radicalisation, and climate-induced insecurities compound the already fragile environment. India, given its geographical location, economic rise, and military capacity, must therefore navigate a uniquely complex security environment while safeguarding its national interests.

Global Geopolitical Realities and Security Challenges Impacting South Asia

South Asia's security is deeply entangled with broader global geopolitical realities. The United States' Indo-Pacific strategy, China's Belt and Road Initiative (BRI), Russia's reorientation towards Asia, and growing Middle Eastern instability all converge in ways that directly impact the region.

Key factors influencing South Asia include:

- Renewed great-power rivalry often described as Cold War 2.0, the U.S. China competition is reshaping alliances and forcing South Asian states into difficult choices.
- China's assertiveness through the BRI, China has extended its presence across South Asia, from Pakistan's Gwadar Port to Sri Lanka's Hambantota, challenging India's regional primacy.

- Russia's repositioning, despite its deepening partnership with China, Russia continues defence cooperation with India while also exploring new openings in Pakistan.
- Technology and space race, Cybersecurity, artificial intelligence, and militarisation of space are redefining the nature of security threats for South Asia.
- Climate change in South Asia is among the world's most climate-vulnerable regions, with rising sea levels, floods, and heat waves posing existential threats.

South Asia: A Complex and Dynamic Region

South Asia is home to nearly a quarter of humanity, with vast ethnic, linguistic, and religious diversity. Its economic disparities, political instability, and fragile governance structures create fertile ground for both internal and external security challenges.

- Demography and development gaps exacerbate radicalisation and migration.
- Cross-border terrorism undermines regional trust and cooperation.
- Resource disputes over water and energy complicate interstate relations.
- Nuclear weapons in India and Pakistan introduce risks of escalation in times of crisis.

While the region holds immense potential for economic integration, persistent mistrust, particularly between India and Pakistan, has repeatedly undermined institutional cooperation through platforms like SAARC.

Security Challenges in South Asia

Terrorism and Radicalisation

Cross-border terrorism, particularly emanating from Pakistan, remains one of India's foremost security concerns. Radicalisation in Afghanistan, Bangladesh, and the Maldives adds to regional instability. Global terror networks find local resonance, exploiting fragile governance and poverty.

Border Disputes

India's unresolved territorial conflicts with both Pakistan and China have led to wars in the past and continue to generate periodic crises, such as the 2017 Doklam standoff and the 2020 Galwan clashes. These disputes carry nuclear escalation risks.

Political Instability

Weak democratic institutions, military dominance in Pakistan, and fragile governance in Afghanistan create persistent instability. This fragility often spills across borders, complicating India's security environment.

Nuclear Rivalry

India and Pakistan's nuclear doctrines are characterised by opacity and mistrust. The possibility of miscalculation remains high, particularly during crises. China's growing nuclear arsenal further exacerbates India's security dilemmas.

Cybersecurity Threats

South Asia faces growing vulnerabilities in cyberspace. India has been the target of repeated state-sponsored cyberattacks, particularly from China and Pakistan, threatening critical infrastructure, banking systems, and defence networks.

Climate Change and Environmental Insecurity

The melting of Himalayan glaciers threatens water security, while rising sea levels endanger Bangladesh and the Maldives. These challenges intersect with migration pressures, resource conflicts, and urban instability.

Regionalism in South Asia: Security Frameworks and Future

SAARC

Although envisioned as a platform for cooperation, SAARC has been paralysed by India–Pakistan rivalry. Its limited institutional capacity and lack of political will have reduced its effectiveness in addressing security concerns.

BIMSTEC

The Bay of Bengal Initiative for Multi-Sectoral Technical and Economic Cooperation (BIMSTEC) has gained traction as an alternative to SAARC, excluding Pakistan while linking South and Southeast Asia. India views BIMSTEC as central to its "Act East" policy.

IORA

The Indian Ocean Rim Association (IORA) is an increasingly important forum for maritime security, blue economy, and disaster management. As global competition intensifies in the Indo-Pacific, IORA's role in promoting regional stability is likely to expand.

The Shanghai Cooperation Organisation (SCO)

India's full membership in 2017 expanded its engagement with Central Asia, Russia, and China. The SCO provides a platform for counterterrorism and energy cooperation, though India remains cautious of China–Pakistan convergence within the organisation.

Future Outlook

Regionalism in South Asia will remain constrained by political mistrust, particularly India–Pakistan tensions. However, subregional and transregional platforms like BIMSTEC and IORA present viable avenues for India to pursue cooperative security initiatives.

Security Challenges of India and Its Strategic Responses

India–Russia Relations

Russia remains India's principal defence partner, providing advanced systems such as the S-400. However, Russia's deepening ties with China and growing engagement with Pakistan pose challenges for India. The future of India–Russia ties will depend on balancing legacy defence cooperation with new geopolitical realities.

India–United States Relations

India–U.S. relations have deepened significantly, particularly in defence, technology, and maritime security. The two countries conduct regular military exercises, collaborate on critical technologies, and coordinate in Indo-Pacific strategies. Yet, India remains cautious of overdependence on Washington.

Strategic Autonomy and Multipolarity

India continues to emphasise "strategic autonomy," seeking to balance relations with multiple major powers rather than align exclusively with any one bloc. This is evident in India's participation in the Quad, BRICS, SCO, and G20 simultaneously.

Military Modernisation

India has invested heavily in modernising its armed forces, enhancing maritime capabilities in the Indian Ocean, and strengthening cyber and space security. Indigenous defence production under the "Atmanirbhar Bharat," initiative is central to reducing dependency on imports.

Diplomacy and Multilateral Engagement

India employs proactive diplomacy to shape regional and global security discourses. Its leadership roles in climate negotiations, counterterrorism initiatives, and Indo-Pacific partnerships demonstrate its growing global influence.

Conclusion

South Asia stands at the crossroads of global geopolitical transformation. For India, the convergence of great-power rivalry, regional instability, and emerging multidimensional threats presents both risks and opportunities.

India must strengthen indigenous defence capacity, deepen regional partnerships (particularly through BIMSTEC and IORA), and continue leveraging its strategic autonomy to balance relations with major powers. As the only state bordering two collusive nuclear adversaries, India's security requires a nuanced combination of deterrence, pragmatic diplomacy, and multilateral engagement.

Ultimately, India's ability to secure its interests will depend on how effectively it navigates the overlapping challenges of terrorism, border disputes, climate change, and technological warfare within an increasingly volatile global order.

REFERENCES

Acharya, A. (2014). The end of American world order. Polity.

Bajpai, K., Basit, S., & Krishnappa, V. (Eds.). (2014). India's grand strategy: History, theory, cases. Routledge.

Buzan, B., & Wæver, O. (2003). Regions and powers: The structure of international security. Cambridge University Press.

Chaudhuri, R. (2018). India and the Asian geopolitics of the twenty-first century. Routledge.

Contessi, N. P. (2016). Foreign and security policy diversification: Comparing China and India. Journal of Strategic Studies, 39(2), 254–288.

Ganguly, Š., & Pardesi, M. S. (2009). Explaining sixty years of India's foreign policy. India Review, 8(1), 4–19.

Hall, I. (2019). Modi and the reinvention of Indian foreign policy. Bristol University Press.

Joshi, M. (2021). Understanding India's national security policy. ORF Occasional Paper.

Kapur, H. (2020). India's foreign policy: Coping with the changing world. SAGE Publications.

Pant, H. V. (2016). Indian foreign policy: An overview. Manchester University Press.

Rakhimov, M. (2010). Central Asia: Regional security and cooperation. Security Index, 16(2), 63–76.

Tellis, A. J. (2020). India's emerging role in the Indo-Pacific. Carnegie Endowment for International Peace.

Wagner, C. (2016). India's policy towards Afghanistan. Stiftung Wissenschaft und Politik.

3

Regional Transport Networks: Silk Route Regionalism and Connectivity Expansion

Nivedita Das Kundu

ABSTRACT

This chapter examines how regional transport networks are revitalizing Silk Route regionalism and reshaping connectivity across Central and South Asia. It outlines the strategic and geo-economic significance of re-connecting historic corridors through contemporary initiatives such as China's Belt and Road Initiative (BRI), TRACECA, the TAPI gas pipeline, the International North South Transport Corridor (INSTC), and the Asian Highway and Trans-Eurasian information links. Focusing especially on Uzbekistan's evolving role and cooperative posture, the chapter surveys rail, road, pipeline, power, and digital corridors and highlights emerging project, from the Central Asian Power System (CAPS) to CASA-1000, TUTAP, and the China–Kyrgyzstan–Uzbekistan (CKU) railway. It also reviews the practical obstacles to seamless connectivity, including physical infrastructure constraints and non-physical barriers (customs, documentation, and border procedures), while noting the potential of policy harmonization and institutional cooperation to ease transit and expand trade. Finally, the chapter emphasizes the normative 'principle of justice, ensuring equitable participation and benefits for all states, as essential to sustainable regional integration and security.

Keywords: *Silk Route regionalism; connectivity; TRACECA; BRI; TAPI; INSTC; CKU railway; CASA-1000; CAPS; Central Asia.*

Introduction

The regional transport networks are expected to improve the network of various routes that for centuries intersected the regional states and generated immense benefits and also promoted cross-cultural concepts. Today, the idea to revive the Silk Route regionalism is also suggesting that all that is needed is to reconnect and retrace old pathways increasing geo-strategic and geopolitical significance of the connectivity. With more investment in equipment and services, better management of facilities and greater intra-regional harmonization, these corridors did show the potential to become important channels of trans-regional transportation hubs. Regional policy makers believes that the Silk Route regionalism projects would not only encourage ties in trade, transport, energy, water resource sharing, but will also promote the spread of democracy and harmony in the region and in the policy making circles this idea is becoming more and more popular. Regarding Uzbekistan's political stance, the country's leader defines it as follows: "When discussing issues related to maintaining stability in Central Asian region through regionalism policies, we cannot overlook such important matters as the rational use of the region's shared water, energy and natural resources. In this regard, we fully support the statement of UN Secretary-General Antonio Guterres that "water, energy, peace, stability issues are closely interconnected."

Major Regional Transport Corridors

Today, in this region exists numerous regional transport network systems, one of the main transport corridor is Central Asia and China's cooperation under the "Belt and Road Initiative" (BRI). Under BRI investment and infrastructure projects are included, collaboration in the energy sector, and the development of trade and economic relations became significant for this regional project. Additionally, China is attempting to strengthen its political ties with the region to further its influence. [1]

TRACECA

Another very important regional transport corridor is Europe-Caucasus-Central Asia corridor (TRACECA). The TRACECA may be referred to as the renaissance of the Great Silk Route. TRACECA is the technical assistance programme for development of the transport corridor between Europe and Asia. The countries of the South Caucasus, the Caspian Sea and the Central Asian countries are involved in the development of this corridor project. In this transport corridor project involves twelve countries Armenia, Azerbaijan,

Bulgaria, Georgia, Kazakhstan, Kyrgyzstan, Moldova, Romania, Tajikistan, Turkey, Uzbekistan and Ukraine. They all signed the basic multilateral agreements for the development of the transport corridor connecting Europe-Caucasus-Central Asia, comprising four supplementary technical annexes on rail and road transport and commercial maritime navigation. TRACECA aims at supporting political and economic independence of all states by enhancing their capacity to access European markets through alternative transport routes, encouraging further regional co-operation among the partner countries. TRACECA helps in assisting in development of economic relations, trade and transport communications in Europe, in the Black Sea region and in Central Asia. It ensures access to the world market ensuring traffic security, cargo safety and environmental protection. TRACECA harmonizes the transport policy and legal structure in the field of transport and creates good conditions for transport cooperation. TRACECA aims for sustainable, efficient and integrated multimodal transport system. [2]

TAPI Energy Corridor

As mentioned before, due to increase in the volume of commercial interactions in the region, many transport corridors are being created. One such energy corridor created is TAPI (Turkmenistan-Afghanistan-Pakistan-India) pipeline. TAPI is envisaged to bring energy from Daulatabad-Herat-Kandahar-Quetta-Multan to Fasilka in the North Indian state of Punjab. This 1800 km. length energy pipeline has got the capacity to carry 90 million metric standard cubic meters gas per day for 30 years. Support of local government and cooperation of all the partners are important to address the security challenges for smooth operations and construction of these corridor projects for the benefit of the larger sections of the regional population.

TAPI is expected to meet the growing energy needs of the regional countries connected with this energy pipeline route. TAPI gas pipeline project has been described by the participant countries as the “Pipeline of Peace” and a “Reflection of Desire”. The TAPI project is expected to bring Central Asia and South Asia much closer to each other. [3] The Dovletabad deposits, which contain 4.5 to 16 thousand cubic meters (tcm) of gas, can supply with the necessary volumes of gas. The 7.6 billion USD, TAPI pipeline first supplies started in the beginning of 2025. Oil and gas firms such as Chevron, Exxon, Gazprom are also part of the project apart from National Oil Companies (NOC) of the participant countries formed a joint venture named TAPI Pipeline Company Limited. [4]

Other Corridors and Power Links

Another significant silk route regionalism transport corridor project is the Asian Highway Network. Another transport corridor project is TASIM (Trans-Eurasian Information Super Highway). Another significant connectivity project is TUTAP. The Central Asian Power System (CAPS), revived in 2022 with Kyrgyzstan and Tajikistan, exemplifies this role, with Uzbekistan exporting 1.5 billion KWh in 2023. Joint hydropower initiatives with Tajikistan Yavan plant (2021). Beyond Central Asia, Uzbekistan exports electricity regularly to Afghanistan, with 300 million kWh supplied in 2023. [5][6][7]

Uzbekistan–Turkmenistan–Iran Transport Corridor

Another railway connectivity project is Railway-line between Uzen (Kazakhstan)-Kyzylkaya-Bereket-Etrek (Turkmenistan)-Gorgan (Iran). The Uzbekistan-Turkmenistan-Iran transport corridor, launched in 2021, enhances regional connectivity, offering access to Persian Gulf ports. [7] Energy cooperation also flourished, with the 2022 CAPS agreement uniting Uzbekistan, Kyrgyzstan, and Tajikistan to share electricity, exporting 1.5 billion kWh in 2023. [5]

International North–South Transport Corridor (INSTC)

Another very significant regional transport corridor is the International North-South Transport Corridor. This project envisages a multi-modal transportation network that connects ports on India's west coast to Bandar Abbas in Iran, then overland to Bandar Anzali. This route reduces transport cost and travel time significantly: Suez route 45–60 days vs. INSTC 25–30 days. The larger implications of the North-South corridor, helping in opening up vast markets of Central Asian region. The politico-economic dimension of these transport corridor routes are significant in the international political scenario with the indications of shift in the global power.

Connectivity Expansion

In the early years after independence, the focus of Central Asian States was mainly on constructing pipelines and developing land-sea transport corridors. As these advanced, other forms of connectivity, aviation, electricity exchange (CASA-1000), and telecommunications (fiber optic backbones) expanded in parallel.

CKU Railway Corridor

The significant transport corridor project connecting China with Kyrgyzstan and Uzbekistan has officially begun construction. After nearly three decades of planning and delays, the CKU rail corridor is now progressing, promising to reduce freight transit times and shorten the China-Europe route by 900 km. [8]

This railway corridor will navigate the challenging terrain of western China and the highest mountains of Kyrgyzstan. The estimated cost is approximately USD 8 billion, potential risks include transit through opium-producing regions. [8]

Trans-Afghan Corridors

In recent times government of Afghanistan has managed to connect with most the Central Asian nations for the development of trans-Afghan transport infrastructure. Mazar-i-Sharif–Herat Kandahar corridor; Spin Boldak Kandahar line; Torghundi Herat; TAT corridor revival; Andkhoy-Sheberghan extensions. [9]

Trade Regimes and Trends

It has been observed that last few years data shows that the trade between the regional countries has shown considerable increase due to the expansion in regional projects and better cooperation. Different trade regimes (CIS, FTA, WTO accessions, bilateral agreements) shape the degree of openness and integration.

Obstacles to Seamless Connectivity

There are obvious problems of geography (mountains, deserts, climate) and man-made obstacles. Physical constraints include deteriorated or mismatched legacy infrastructure, rolling stock shortages, container deficits, and gauge breaks (1520 mm vs. 1435 mm). Non-physical hurdles include visa difficulties for drivers, documentation burdens, customs delays, unsynchronized border post hours, and intermittent political tensions causing closures. Harmonization of procedures and increased use of sealed containers can help mitigate these issues. International training and technical assistance are underway; all Central Asian states have joined the TIR convention and signed multiple bilateral treaties.

Principle of Justice in Regionalism

The principle of justice plays a key role in ensuring the rights of each participating state to equitable benefits. Regionalism policies in Central Asia seek to balance growth with social justice, strengthening civil society and regional stability. Justice implies integrity, restraint, and compassion, and provides a normative foundation for cooperative frameworks.

Conclusion

There is a competitive advantage in Silk Route Regionalism initiative. Cooperation across transport, trade, and connectivity can strengthen the region's role in the global arena, support sustainable development, and elevate well-being. While obstacles persist, pragmatic diplomacy, economic coordination, and security confidence-building can unlock the benefits of an interconnected Eurasia.

REFERENCES

1. Air Power Asia / ResearchGate, "The Belt and Road Initiative (BRI) shown in a world map basis," accessed via ResearchGate.
2. TRACECA programme documents and STRA.TEG library resources on Europe-Caucasus-Asia corridor.
3. Kundu, D. N. (2015). Discussions on the TAPI pipeline as a symbol of 'Pipeline of Peace'.
4. Kundu, D. N., Yulak, M., & Humbatov, M. (2014, September). Notes on TAPI project stakeholders, NOCs, and joint venture 'TAPI Pipeline Company Limited'.
5. International Energy Agency (2023). Data on Uzbekistan/CAPS and regional power exchanges.
6. Radio Free Europe/Radio Liberty (2022). Reporting on Yavan hydropower cooperation and related agreements.
7. World Bank (2024). Uzbekistan power exports; Uzbekistan–Turkmenistan–Iran corridor initiatives.
8. Syed Fazl-e-Haider (Jan 27, 2025). "The CKU corridor: a Silk Road domino," NATO Defense College Foundation coverage and related reports.
9. Umarova (Jan 31, 2025). Analyses of Trans-Afghan corridors (TAT, Five Nation Railway Route) and evolving regional positions.

4

Process of Regionalism in Central Asia

Sharaf Agabayev

ABSTRACT

This article examines the expansion of regional cooperation in Central Asia within the framework of globalization. It highlights the advancement of political dialogue, joint programs and projects in trade, investment, transport and logistics, energy, and agriculture, as well as addressing environmental issues and strengthening cultural and humanitarian activities. These efforts are emphasized as essential foundations for ensuring socio-political stability in the region. The study further demonstrates that the concept of regionalization, defined as the process of developing cooperation in economic, political, cultural, and security spheres within a specific geographical area, is explained through theories such as neofunctionalism, intergovernmentalism, and constructivism. It also explores the establishment of regional organizations, norms, and cooperation mechanisms, as well as the dynamics of regional issues at different levels, ranging from free trade zones to political alliances.

Keywords: *Concept of regionalism; regional culture; politics; economics; geopolitics; globalization; ecology; investment; cooperation; sustainable development; regional identity; regional leadership.*

Historical Background

Central Asia has historically served as a crossroads of civilizations, where diverse peoples and cultures converged. Over millennia, the region witnessed the rise and flourishing of powerful empires and states. In the 20th century, the incorporation of Central Asia into the Soviet Union represented a distinct stage in its political evolution. During this period, national borders were drawn and modern political institutions established; however, opportunities for independent political development remained limited.

The dissolution of the Soviet Union in 1991 ushered in a new era for Central Asia. Five independent republics, Uzbekistan, Kazakhstan, Turkmenistan, Kyrgyzstan, and Tajikistan, emerged, embarking on paths toward sovereignty. In the early years of independence, these states faced complex challenges: consolidating national statehood, initiating economic reforms, building political institutions, and securing distinct positions in the international arena. Each pursued its own political trajectory, resulting in varied models of development across the region.

The stability and progress of Central Asia are crucial not only for regional but also for global stability. Cooperation among its peoples, who have lived in harmony for centuries, remains vital. As Islam Karimov, the first President of Uzbekistan, emphasized:

> "History is driven forward not by conflicts and hostility, but by cooperation and trust between peoples." (Karimov I.A., O'zbekiston XXI asr bo'sag'asida: xavfsizlikka tahdid, barqarorlik shartlari va taraqqiyot kafolatlari. Tashkent: O'zbekiston, 1997, p.323.)

Regionalization in Contemporary Central Asia

In recent years, regionalization processes have intensified, giving rise to new forms of interstate cooperation, integration initiatives, approaches to ensuring regional stability, and strategies for geopolitical evolution. Each Central Asian state possesses distinct advantages: Kazakhstan dominates in land area and economic indicators, Uzbekistan stands out with its population size, Turkmenistan holds vast natural gas reserves, while Kyrgyzstan and Tajikistan are rich in hydro-energy potential due to their mountainous geography.

Regionalization in Central Asia is best understood as a multidimensional process of geopolitical, geoeconomic, and cultural-humanitarian integration. It entails the institutionalization of interstate cooperation, the strengthening of regional identity, and the consolidation of the region into a coherent complex. Both external and internal factors shape this process, sometimes functioning as tools for external influence, also as mechanisms to secure stability and security.

In the context of modern global processes, regionalization reflects growing interdependence, deepening integration, and the creation of regional institutions and mechanisms. It strengthens Central Asia's position in the international arena, facilitates conflict resolution, and enables collective responses to shared challenges. Political, economic, cultural, humanitarian, and security cooperation are all expanding, evidenced by regular summits of regional leaders, high-level meetings, and joint projects, which underscore that regional integration has entered a new phase.

Uzbekistan's President Shavkat Mirziyoyev mentioned:

> "We are bound together by a shared history and culture, a common sacred religion, similar mentalities, moral and ethical values, traditions, and an inseparable friendship. All of this serves as a strong foundation for mutually beneficial cooperation aimed at uniting the potential of Central Asian states for the prosperity and well-being of our peoples." (Mirziyoyev Sh., Speech at the Second Consultative Meeting of Central Asian Leaders, Tashkent, November 29, 2019).

Stages of Regionalization

The regionalization of Central Asia can be divided into distinct stages:

- 1991–2000: The formative period, marked by independence, the establishment of national statehood, and the need for cooperation mechanisms.
- 2000–2010: The creation of regional organizations, security cooperation, and early integration efforts.
- 2010–2020: The revision of regional strategies, the emergence of new cooperation formats, and the strengthening of bilateral relations.
- 2020–Present: A renewed phase of active cooperation, intensified regional engagement, and consolidation of regional identity.

These stages illustrate the evolving dynamics of regionalization, shaped by internal political developments, external factors, and the strategic priorities of the states involved. Uzbekistan's proactive policy of fostering friendly relations with its neighbours has given new impetus to cooperation, institutionalization, and problem-solving mechanisms.

Regional Institutions and External Partners

Regional institutions serve as the structural backbone of integration. They regulate interstate cooperation, address common challenges, and reflect the region's geopolitical priorities. Notable examples include:

- Central Asian Cooperation (CAC) (est. 2002): focused on trade, economic ties, energy, and transport.
- Shanghai Cooperation Organization (SCO) (est. 2001): emphasizing security, counterterrorism, and economic collaboration.
- Eurasian Economic Union (EAEU) (est. 2014): promoting economic integration and the free movement of goods, services, and labor.

Central Asia's relations with external partners also play a defining role:

- Russia: historical, political, and economic integration;
- China: Belt and Road Initiative projects;
- United States (C5+1 format): security, development, and democratic reforms;
- European Union: legal and institutional reforms, modernization, and human rights.

Regular consultative meetings among Central Asian leaders since 2018 have institutionalized cooperation further, producing action plans, agreements on security, trade, and energy, and fostering cultural and environmental cooperation.

Key Dimensions of Regional Cooperation

- Trade and Economy: Significant increases in intra-regional trade, reductions in barriers, and interdependence in agriculture, textiles, energy, and construction materials.
- Energy: Complementary resources but challenges in water, energy balance, pricing, and transportation, requiring negotiated solutions.

- Transport and Logistics: Major infrastructure initiatives like the Belt and Road Initiative, TRACECA, and the North-South Corridor seek to overcome the region's landlocked geography.
- Security and Water Resources: Managing shared rivers (Amu Darya, Syr Darya) is vital for stability, with recent progress in cooperation.
- Environmental Security: Programs address air quality, biodiversity, waste management, disaster response, and the green economy.
- Cultural and Humanitarian Ties: Shared heritage strengthens regional identity; cooperation in education, youth exchanges, healthcare, and science is expanding.

Regional Identity and Leadership

Regional identity stems from shared history, culture, language, and values, but faces challenges as national identities consolidate. Strengthening this identity could enhance cooperation and stability. Leadership dynamics also shape integration. Kazakhstan's economic power and Uzbekistan's demographic and geographic advantages position them as leading actors. In recent years, competition has given way to cooperation, producing a more balanced and constructive regional dynamic.

Conclusion

Regionalism in Central Asia is an evolving, multifaceted process influenced by internal and external dynamics. Since independence in 1991, the region has progressed from fragmented beginnings toward structured integration. Today, deeper cooperation in politics, economy, security, transport, environment, and culture is both a necessity and a strategic imperative.

Future priorities include expanding political dialogue, improving institutional mechanisms, enhancing trade and transport connectivity, balancing water and energy resources, fostering cultural, humanitarian ties, and embracing digital transformation, innovation, and green economy principles. These developments will not only secure sustainable growth and strengthen the region's international standing but also improve the welfare of its peoples.

REFERENCES

1. Karimov I.A. O'zbekiston XXI asr bo'sag'asida: xavfsizlikka tahdid, barqarorlik shartlari va taraqqiyot kafolatlari. – T.: O'zbekiston. 1997. - B.323. https://president.uz/oz/lists/view/6660
2. Sh. Mirziyoyev. "Markaziy Osiyo davlatlari rahbarlarining ikkinchi Maslahat uchrashuvi". Toshkent. 2019 yil, 29-noyabr.
3. Markaziy Osiyo rahbarlarining Olmaota uchrashuvida "Markaziy Osiyo hamkorligi" (MOH) tashkilotini tuzish haqidagi Shartnomasi. 2002-yil, 28-fevral. https://uz.wikipedia.org/wiki/Markaziy_Osiyo_hamkorligi_tashkiloti
Shanxay hamkorlik tashkiloti (SHHT) - Xitoyning Shanxay shahrida 6 mamlakat – Qozog'iston, Xitoy, Qirg'iziston, Rossiya, Tojikiston va O'zbekiston davlat rahbarlari uchrashuvida tuzilgan. 2001 yil, 15-iyun. https://uz.wikipedia.org/wiki/ Shanxay_ hamkorlik_tashkiloti
4. Yevroosiyo Iqtisodiy Ittifoqi (YOII) – 29-may 2014-yilda tashkil etilgan. https://uz.wikipedia.org/wiki/Yevrosiyo_iqtisodiy_ittifoqi
O'zbekiston Respublikasi Prezidenti Shavkat Mirziyoyevning Birlashgan Millatlar Tashkiloti Bosh Assambleyasining 72-sessiyasida so'zlagan nutqi. 2017 yil, 19-sentabr.
https://davr24.uz/archives/3261
https://uz.wikipedia.org/wiki/Bir_makon_bir_yo%CA%BBl_tashabbusi
https://uz.wikipedia.org/wiki/C5%2B1
https://tashcoe.uwed.uz/wp-content/uploads/2022/07/YeIning_Markaziy_Osiyo_boyicha_Yangi_strategiyasi_Ozbek_tilida.pdf
https://president.uz/oz/lists/view/1571
https://president.uz/oz/3093
https://president.uz/oz/lists/view/4530
https://president.uz/oz/lists/view/5350
https://uza.uz/oz/posts/markaziy-osiyo-davlatlari-rahbarlarining-beshinchi-maslahat-uchrashuvi-umummintaqaviy-xavfsizlik-shakllanadi_520360
https://uz.wikipedia.org/wiki/Janubi-Sharqiy_Osiyo_davlatlari_uyushmasi
5. Sirojov O. Markaziy Osiyo mintaqasida hamkorlik jarayonlari (tajriba va istiqbol). B-204.
Yevropa-Kavkaz-Osiyo transport yo'lagi, TRACECA - Yevropani Kavkaz orkali Osiyo bilan bog'laydigan avtomobil va temir yo'llari majmui. https://uz.wikipedia.org/wiki/Yevropa-Kavkaz-Osiyo_transport_yo%CA%BBlagi
6. O'zbekiston Respublikasi Prezidentining "O'zbekiston Respublikasini yanada rivojlantirish bo'yicha Harakatlar strategiyasi to'g'risida" Farmoni PF-4947-son. Toshkent, 2017 yil, 7-fevral.
7. Первая консультативная встреча глав государств Центральной Азии. Электронный ресурс. URL: https://uza.uz/ru/posts/pervaya-konsultativnaya-vstrecha-glav-gosudarstv-tsentralnoy-15-03-2018. (дата обращения: 22.03.2025).
8. Саммит глав государств Центральной Азии в Ташкенте придаст новый импульс региональной интеграции. Электронный ресурс. URL: https://www.newscentralasia.net/2019/12/02/central-asia-summit-tashkent-ru/. (дата обращения: 22.03.2025).
9. В Туркменистане прошла третья консультативная встреча президентов стран Центральной Азии. Электронный ресурс. URL: https://www.

trtavaz.com.tr/haber/rus/avrasyadan/v-turkmenistane-proshla-tretya-konsultativnaya-vstrecha-prezidentov-stran-tsen/610d322601a30a1c28ae1434. (дата обращения: 22.03.2025).
10. Президент Узбекистана выступил за повышение эффективности многостороннего сотрудничества в регионе. Электронный ресурс. URL: https://president.uz/ru/lists/view/5357. (дата обращения: 22.03.2025).
11. В Душанбе прошла Пятая консультативная встреча глав государств Центральной Азии. Электронный ресурс. URL: https://cis.minsk.by/news/26058/v_dushanbe_proshla_pjataja_konsultativnaja_vstrecha_glav_gosudarstv_centralnoj_azii (дата обращения: 22.03.2025).
12. Крупнейшие месторождения Казахстана. Электронный ресурс. URL: https://dprom.kz/dobycha/krupnejshie-mestorozhdeniya-kazahstana/ (дата обращения: 13.03.2025).
9. Природные ресурсы. Электронный ресурс. URL: https://dev-portal.miit.uz/ru/why-uzbekistan/natural-resources (дата обращения: 21.03.2025).
14. В шести областях Узбекистана нашли новые месторождения урана. Электронный ресурс. URL: https://tass.ru/ekonomika/21799409 (дата обращения: 21.03.2025).
15. Энергетическая политика Туркменистана: важность и перспективы газопровода ТАПИ. Электронный ресурс. URL: https://www.eurasian-research.org/publi cation/energy-policies-of-turkmenistan-importance-and-perspectives-of-tapi-natural-gas-pipeline/. (дата обращения: 21.03.2025).
16. О Кыргызской Республике. Электронный ресурс. URL: https://invest.gov.kg/ru/. (дата обращения: 21.03.2025).
17. Гидроэнергетические ресурсы Таджикистана. Электронный ресурс. URL: https://www.mewr.tj/?page_id=614#:~:text=%. (дата обращения: 21.03.2025).
18. Маркова Е.А. Энергетическая политика стран Центральной Азии: основные итоги. Проблемы постсоветского пространства. 2020;7(3):365-372. https://doi.org/10.24 975/2313-8920-2020-7-3-365-372).
19. Торгово-экономическое сотрудничество стран Центральной Азии. Электронный ресурс. URL: https://www.cer.uz/en/post/publication/torgovo-ekonomiceskoe-sotrudnicestvo-stran-centralnoj-azii-v-period-pandemii. (дата обращения: 22.03.2025).

5

The Soft Power Factor in the Foreign Policy of Uzbekistan

Sanjar Saidov

ABSTRACT

This Chapter analyzes the foundations, principles and features of the use of "soft power" in the modern foreign policy of Uzbekistan. Based on the theory of "soft power", its normative, institutional and personnel aspects are revealed. The main contour of Uzbekistan's "soft power" is primarily the Central Asian region. Following the election of Shavkat Mirziyoyev as President of Uzbekistan, regional integration based on mutual cooperation and strategic partnership has been revived in Central Asia. As a single regional entity, Central Asia has opened a broad path for full participation in modern international relations. In this regard, along with bilateral and multilateral relations at the state level, cooperation between the peoples of the region is growing as a constant trend. The national, religious and cultural unity of Central Asia, the common goals and hopes of our peoples are pushing them towards unity in political terms. In these processes, first of all, Uzbekistan is entrusted with a huge historical mission. Using its soft power potential, Uzbekistan must strengthen its position as a responsible leader in Central Asia. It is these issues that are scientifically analyzed in this Chapter.

Keywords: *"Soft power", Uzbekistan, Central Asia, foreign policy, reforms, cooperation and democracy.*

Introduction

In today's world, the quality aspects of international relations are gaining new content and significance. The emergence of new actors in foreign policy is accompanied by the refinement of its principles, strategies, and tactics. Globalization and the widespread use of digital technologies are enhancing this trend, assigning modern tasks to states, international organizations, multinational companies, and alliances. Undoubtedly, one of these trends is the phenomenon of "soft power."

The manifestation of geopolitical processes at the global and regional level in new and complex forms requires each country to modify its domestic and foreign policies. In such conditions, the changing system of the world order and the formation of new geostrategic realities require strengthening regional and international cooperation, based on national interests. These trends are directly related to the "soft power" factor, which includes the strengthening of the state's image and the growth of political motivation. These processes are acquiring current significance not only from a scientific and conceptual point of view, but also from the point of view of strengthening the role of Uzbekistan within the framework of cooperation in Central Asia.

Origin and Theoretical aspects of the Category "soft power"

"Soft power" differs from "hard power," which relies on coercion, by its ability to achieve any results based on voluntary participation, sympathy, and attractiveness. In recent years, the term "soft power" has frequently appeared in public media, as well as, in the speeches of various experts in the fields of political science and sociology. The concept of "soft power" first emerged in the late twentieth century in the work of American political scientist Joseph Nye (Bound to Lead: The Changing Nature of American Power).[1] According to Nye, the policy of soft power has become one of the important trends in modern foreign policy of leading states. Later, he further developed this category in his 2004 book, "Soft Power: The Means to Success in World Politics."[2]

In our view, the practical application of "soft power" in political processes is a relatively recent phenomenon, primarily applied in the last two centuries. The experience of exerting cultural influence in the international relations system, which is currently gaining widespread recognition, has been present in a unique form for many centuries. It is essential to emphasize the hypothesis that soft power, as a policy of enhancing voluntary actions through cultural appeal, has always been utilized not only alongside "hard power" but also distinctly with its own methods and diversity.

This natural question arises: *why does humanity always turn to political events referred to as "soft power"?* In the context of human nature, an explanation is possible. In human nature, the resolution of issues is not only possible through military force but also through the power of words.

As the ancient Roman philosopher Cicero emphasized: "There are two types of activities that can elevate the value of a person to the highest degree: military prowess or intellectual distinction. The former defends against enemy threats, while the latter ensures peace and stability in the state. For the complete prosperity of the state, an alliance of sword and pen is necessary".[3]

Similarly, in the works of the Italian thinker Niccolo Machiavelli, it is argued that any state must conduct its politics in such a way that its subjects should fear and love their ruler at the same time, according to Machiavelli. According to Machiavelli's philosophy, there are two ways to achieve a goal through action: the path of law (resembling the human path) and the path of force (resembling the animal path). However, the legal path is often less effective.[4] Therefore, people sometimes resort to the second method. Rulers, in Machiavelli's view, should be knowledgeable about both human and animal nature, developing and utilizing both methods in a similar manner. For this reason, rulers should resemble two animals the lion and the fox.

Institutionalization of "soft power"

Soft power is not only the possibilities and advantages for voluntary actions but also a combination of institutions, standards, and rules that attract attention and are implemented by other actors. Such standards, institutions, and structures form the integral framework of soft power, mainly based on three primary sources: *the cultural heritage and appealing aspects of a nation for others; the system of political values accepted by the international community; and the external political model based on legitimacy and anchored in ethical principles.*

However, "soft power" also has its limitations and boundaries similar to "hard power." How are they described? The constraints of hard power, for example, are represented by the conventional weapons of mass destruction, primarily nuclear weapons, and the deadly consequences they pose. "Hard power", restrains itself due to its degree of severity. How are the boundaries of soft power delineated? Centuries of political history demonstrate that the diffusion and impact of soft power, through a system of rules, are influenced by the geographical boundaries of the region managed by an actor and the neighboring areas with which it interacts. For instance, the Hellenistic Empire of Alexander the Great did not extend beyond the limits of the Macedonian homeland, but Roman civilization influenced its boundaries and the civilizations of neighboring states through a system of established rules. Even though the British had colonies on five continents, they mainly preserved them through military means, and ultimately, this approach led to the gradual decline of this power in a predetermined manner.

The concept of cultural-hegemonic dominance, which played a fundamental role in the formation of the "soft power" phenomenon, can be traced back to the writings of the Italian philosopher Antonio Gramsci in the 1930s. This concept was developed in his work "Prison Notebooks" (Quaderni del carcere) and has served as a foundation, arguably. The said work quickly gained prominence, particularly among neo-conservatives in Western Europe and America.[5]

It should be emphasized that understanding soft power merely as a non-military method of achieving objectives and influence is overly simplistic and lacks nuance. This perspective does not allow for genuine exploration of events, and it fails to establish clear delimitative boundaries. Therefore, if soft power is solely considered as a non-military method for achieving goals, natural questions arise: *Is the ideological struggle between two antagonists considered a visible manifestation of soft power in relation to each other? Can religious teachings or religious organizations be regarded as specific forms of soft power acting as social institutions?* Undoubtedly, within the broad definition provided earlier, providing precise answers to these questions is challenging.

Consequently, further research into soft power necessitates a more precise and effective approach. According to J. Nye's definition, there are three types of power in the political system: (1) coercive power (asserting and applying influence through hard power); (2)

incentivizing power (gaining influence through money and material resources); and (3) soft power or cultural influence (attracting others to one's own preferred direction voluntarily).[6] In this context, cultural influence, which involves the voluntary acceptance of a particular perspective by an active actor, clarifies the essence of the concept of soft power more distinctly.

Edward Carr, a British historian and international relations researcher, expressed his views on cultural influence on the international stage almost half a century before Nye. Carr divided the power factor into three categories: military, economic, and "power over ideas (dominance)." Notably, Carr's writings on "power over ideas" in 1939 coincided with the rise of fascism and Nazism, which were casting their shadows over all of Europe and civilization at that time.[7]

Indeed, the emergence and widespread dissemination of fascism initially involved the establishment of "dominance over ideas." It is crucial to emphasize that history consists of repetitions. Many historical events can manifest themselves in new forms and expressions under contemporary conditions.

The two devastating world wars that occurred in the 20th century, the proliferation of weapons of mass destruction, and other factors underscored the inadequacy of resolving contentious issues through military means. They demonstrated the increasing significance of non-military methods, including economic, ideological, and cultural influence, in international relations. As a result, understanding the mechanisms of non-military influence and recognizing their substantial efficacy have led to revisiting the misconceptions of previous generations that favored the superiority of hard power over soft power.

The Structure of "soft power"

The effectiveness of implementing the soft power policy is determined by three crucial factors: *organizational and institutional* foundations (identifying the strategy and main directions of soft power; selecting and supporting implementing institutions); *information and cultural* capacity (forming a conceptual and ideological narrative; creating a positive information environment relative to oneself; conducting public opinion monitoring, etc.); and the *personnel system* (having specialists capable of implementing soft power political analysts, international relations experts, image-makers, poli-technologists, and others).

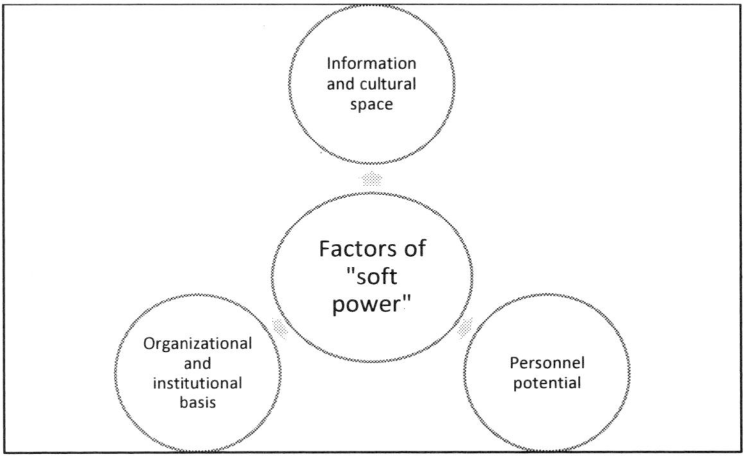

In today's world, nearly all countries are inclined to benefit from soft power policies as a subject of international relations. However, its application is not universal and effective for everyone. For instance, the international organization Portland-PR regularly researches and announces the rankings of various countries' utilization of soft power. The Soft Power Index[8] rating only includes about 30 countries, indicating that they effectively utilize soft power in their foreign policies.

In these indices, the main instruments of soft power diplomacy, such as political PR, information campaigns, global marketing, the global dominance of the state language, the state's position in the global hierarchy, cultural exchange, sports, tourism, public diplomacy, education system, information wars, intercultural dialogue, national diasporas, and migration policies, are assessed.

Some aspects of "soft power" of Uzbekistan

In recent years, there is a growing trend of active participation in regional politics, regional and global integration processes in Uzbekistan. The Strategy for Actions on the five priority areas of development of the Republic of Uzbekistan in 2021-2026, in the section 5.2., emphasizes the need to strengthen the country's international influence and enhance the activities in the field of global information delivery, among other priorities.[9]

Additionally, the Presidential Decree of January 18, 2017, "On additional measures to further enhance the activities of diplomatic missions of the Republic of Uzbekistan abroad," and the Concept of the State Policy of the Republic of Uzbekistan in the Field of International Relations, adopted on November 15, 2019, as well as the currently discussed "Concept for strengthening Uzbekistan's positive image in the international arena," are significant normative-legal documents in this regard.

However, this is only one aspect of the issue. To effectively implement the soft power in international relations, Uzbekistan needs to consider what it should pay attention to or take into account. Answering questions like, "*Can Uzbekistan effectively utilize the soft power factor, and to what extent*?", requires a nuanced approach. In this context, analyzing several aspects is essential:

Firstly, the actor who wants to implement the soft power policy must initially define its geographical boundaries (global or regional). As a developing country on the path to progress, Uzbekistan's soft power potential is undoubtedly centered in the Central Asian region. Its role as a collaborator and integrator in Central Asia is crucial. Thus, Uzbekistan's geographical centrality and equality with all five neighboring states serve as fundamental factors. Currently, the political leadership of Uzbekistan is dealing with various boundary issues (delimitation and demarcation), which are unresolved territorial problems. In the future, direct consultations between the leadership of Uzbekistan, which has embarked on Central Asian diplomacy with determination, could be an effective instrument. These "consultations" could serve not only Uzbekistan's but also the entire region's geopolitical interests.

Secondly, it is evident that the Afghanistan factor plays a significant role in Uzbekistan's recent regional foreign policy. The international conference on "Cooperation and Regional Partnership in Ensuring Security and Sustainable Development" dedicated to Afghan issues, held in Tashkent in March 2018, and successful talks with the leadership of the Taliban movement in Tashkent from August 7 to 10, 2019, demonstrate country's active involvement in addressing

Afghan issues. These diplomatic efforts can be evaluated as a successful page in Uzbekistan's foreign policy, contrasting with the "Moscow format" negotiations under the leadership of Russia and the "SCO + Afghanistan" dialogue initiated by China. Uzbekistan's active participation in the economic and social development of Afghanistan, as well as collaboration in education and culture, positively contributes to its image.[10] Currently, Uzbekistan is required to maintain its leadership role in stabilizing and developing Afghanistan and aligning it with the Central Asian integration orbit.

Thirdly, it is essential to recognize the importance of the national identity and language factor in the soft power policy. The Uzbek language, its rich lexicon, and corpus have been topics of extensive discussion. Now, the time has come to actively use this factor. According to statistical data, Uzbeks make up more than 3 million in Afghanistan, over 1.3 million in Tajikistan, over 918 thousand in Kyrgyzstan, more than 576 thousand in Kazakhstan, and over 250 thousand in Turkmenistan. The Uzbek language, being the official language of Uzbekistan and Afghanistan, holds local significance in other Central Asian countries as well.

Due to certain subjective reasons, we have established close ties with our fellow countrymen during a specific period. Today, it is crucial to strengthen cultural ties, promote the learning of the Uzbek language, and expand broadcasting aimed at Uzbek speakers. In this regard, it is necessary to make effective use of the experience of leading countries, such as Germany's Goethe Institute, France's "Alliance Française," and projects like Russia's "Russkiy mir."

Fourthly, Uzbekistan has the potential to become a "cultural and tourist hub" and a "hub of education" in Central Asia. Uzbekistan has five tangible cultural heritage sites and eight intangible cultural heritage elements included in UNESCO's World Heritage List.[11] Cities such as Samarkand, Bukhara, Khiva, Kokand, Shakhrisabz, and Termez serve not only as Uzbekistan's but also as the cultural heritage of all Central Asian peoples. Therefore, it is important to boost tourism, grant privileges to citizens in the region, and consider the strategic goal of achieving 10 tangible and more than 5 intangible cultural heritage elements by 2030.

Moreover, it is essential to recognize that the most effective instrument of “soft power” is supporting non-governmental organizations (NGOs). Countries with successful soft power strategies support the development of NGO sectors both globally and locally through grants for social projects and initiatives. In Uzbekistan, the Parliament’s Foundation for Supporting NGOs, under the Oliy Majlis, should enhance its capabilities, and national NGOs need to improve their fundraising strategies.

Additionally, the establishment of strong media and information infrastructures is crucial. Uzbekistan should aim to create a single information space throughout Central Asia, not only relying on traditional but also modern public information and communication networks.

Furthermore, the utilization of “soft power” requires an emphasis on human resources. At present, Uzbekistan needs to develop modern knowledge and technologies, recruit active and dynamic young professionals, and apply strategic goals such as the transformation of its foreign policy philosophy towards smart power. If we analyze the issue from the perspective of the compatibility of regional interests, the shared cultural values, friendship, and brotherhood among the people, the unity of language, and the harmony of religious and spiritual values can be considered crucial factors for Uzbekistan to exert a unique influence on the global community as a form of “soft power”.

For example, the renowned American scholar Frederik Starr, in his book “Lost Enlightenment: Central Asia’s Golden Age from the Arab Conquest to Tamerlane,” elaborates on the glorious period of Central Asia, which serves as an inspiring source and spiritual wealth for all peoples of the region. From a regional perspective, the shared historical heritage emphasizes unity and mutual understanding among the nations.[12]

Utilizing “soft power” effectively in international relations requires timely and relevant responses to the soft influences of other geopolitical actors. For instance, the critical remarks made by Maria Zakharova, the official representative of the Russian Ministry of Foreign Affairs, regarding the draft law on conducting official affairs in the state language in Uzbekistan in May 2020 and the subsequent broad public and official reactions emphasize the necessity of continuous attention to these matters.

Another case worth mentioning is Russia's introduction of a new type of radio-electronic warfare missile system along its northern and western borders in 2018. The fact that this new missile system was named "Samarqand" is not only an issue for us but also a matter of global significance. Samarqand, being not just the city but a globally renowned city in the Muslim world, symbolizes not war and aggression but peace, knowledge, and science. Uzbekistan's official authorities responded to this incident with silence. Unfortunately, using the name (brand) without obtaining the consent of its author would be considered an unlawful act even if it were beneficial.

Conclusion

In conclusion, Uzbekistan, to successfully participate in the "soft power" market, needs to possess significant cultural, artistic, scientific, literary, cinematographic, tourist, culinary, as well as economic, infrastructural, transport-logistic capabilities. This will serve the important goal of ensuring organic unity among the peoples of Central Asia and bearing responsible leadership tasks in the region.

In summary, it should be emphasized that "soft power" and political image instruments are, firstly, integral elements of a country's economic, political, social, and cultural potential. Although they are crucial, they represent only a part of the equation. The real influence lies not just in symbolic expressions but in tangible realities. For Uzbekistan to effectively execute its regional policy using "soft power," it is essential not only to utilize the potential in economic, political, social, and cultural spheres but also to implement substantial democratic reforms. Uzbekistan should not imitate democracy in its domestic policies but rather strive to implement genuine democratic values. Only by doing so can Uzbekistan reach its full potential in the regional power balance.

It is also necessary to institutionally and qualitatively reform the foreign policy of Uzbekistan. It is advisable to accept the updated "Concept of Foreign Policy Activities of the Republic of Uzbekistan" as a document open to the public, enriching it with new functions of political management characteristic of the 21st century.

REFERENCES

1. Nye, J. (1990). Bound to lead: The changing nature of American power. New York: Basic Books.
2. Nye, Joseph S., Jr. (2005). Soft Power: The Means to Success in World Politics. Public Affairs Books. Copy at http://www.tinyurl.com/mug36ku
3. Marcus Tullius Cicero/Speeches (Цицерон Марк Туллий. «Речи». В 2-х т. т. I-II. Изд-во академии наук СССР, М., 1962. С. 30)
4. Sovereign Niccolo Machiavelli / "Gosudar" Nikkolo Makiavelli, Softcover, 2002. -P. 85.
5. Antonio Gramsci. Prison Notebooks // https://abahlali.org/files/gramsci.pdf
6. Nye Jr. Joseph S. Soft Power. The Means to Success in World Politics. First ed. New York: Public Affairs, 2004. P. 2.
7. Carr Edward Hallet. The Twenty Years' Crisis 1919-1939. New York: Palgrave, 2001. p. 102.
8. The soft power index. https://softpower30.com/
9. Decree of the President of the Republic of Uzbekistan "On the development strategy of Uzbekistan for 2022-2026". // https://lex.uz/docs/5841077
10. In 2017, a secondary specialized educational institution began operating in the Termez district of the Surkhandarya region, designed to educate Afghan youth.
11. UNESCO Office in Uzbekistan // http://www.unesco.org/new/ru/Tashkent Lost Enlightenment: Central Asia's Golden Age from the Arab Conquest to Tamerlane. S.
12. Frederick Starr. Princeton University Press. October 2013.

6

China's Strategic Focus and Role in the Shanghai Cooperation Organization

Kulaisha Nazarova, Dinara Dauyen, and Erkin Baidarov

ABSTRACT

In the context of the constantly evolving global geopolitical landscape, the Shanghai Cooperation Organization (SCO) demands close analysis, particularly with respect to its strategic orientations and the pivotal role of China within this multilateral platform. This chapter undertakes a comprehensive examination of the SCO's prospects and trends, with special emphasis on identifying strategic priorities and assessing the impact of Chinese policy on multilateral cooperation. The scientific significance of this chapter lies in its integrated approach to evaluate China's foreign policy strategy, economic diplomacy, and technological influence on regional cooperation. The practical contribution is the development of policy recommendations designed to optimize and strengthen the role of the SCO in international affairs.

Methodologically, the research employs analytical review, comparative analysis, case study, SWOT analysis, and scenario planning. This multidimensional approach allows for an objective assessment of the dynamics and vectors shaping multilateral cooperation within the SCO. The study reveals the strengthening of China's influence within the SCO, primarily manifested through deepening economic ties and infrastructure development. At the same time, the Organization faces challenges arising from the heterogeneity of member state's interests and external geopolitical pressures. To address these, China has introduced a series of strategic initiatives. This chapter contributes to the understanding of international relations in the Eurasian region and enriches academic discourse by analyzing current SCO trends. The practical value lies in the formulation of strategic recommendations aimed at enhancing the effectiveness of multilateral cooperation and promoting deeper integration across various dimensions of the Organization's activities.

Keywords: *Cooperation, Politics, States, International Relations, Territory, Strategy, Investment.*

Introduction

Established in 2001, the Shanghai Cooperation Organization (SCO) is a multilateral alliance that includes China, Russia, and several other Asian states. Over the past two decades, the SCO has assumed an important role in advancing regional security and economic development. Among its members, China, both a founding state and a principal actor, has been particularly influential in shaping the Organization's policies and initiatives, placing significant emphasis on strengthening cooperation.

Relevance

In an era defined by shifting world orders and the growing prominence of economic and political blocs, the relevance of examining multilateral regional organizations such as the SCO is particularly acute. The SCO represents a distinctive model of trans-regional cooperation, especially as China's influence in international relations continues to expand. Analyzing China's approach to the SCO not only provides insight into Chinese policy but also sheds light on broader transformations in international security and economic cooperation across Asia. Although numerous studies have explored aspects of the SCO's activities, comprehensive research focusing specifically on China's role and contributions remains limited. Given that China is a central actor in determining the strategy and trajectory of the SCO, this gap underscores the importance of the present study.

Research Problem, Object, and Subject

The object of this study is the SCO as a regional international organization within the broader context of international relations. The subject is the SCO's activities, with particular focus on the Chinese approach and its influence. The research problem emerges from the dynamic evolution of international relations and the changing priorities of Chinese foreign policy, which present both challenges and opportunities for the SCO. Divergent member-state interests, coupled with external pressures such as geopolitical rivalries and economic sanctions, further complicate the Organization's cohesion. Understanding China's dominant role is essential for assessing how the SCO can adapt to these challenges and what long-term consequences may arise from Chinese policy.

Novelty of the Research

This study is distinguished by its focus on analyzing China's strategic approach to the SCO in light of the latest foreign policy trends, including the "One Belt, One Road" (BRI) initiative. Viewing the SCO through the prism of China's economic projects and regional initiatives offers a new scientific perspective, enriching the understanding of Chinese foreign policy and its strategic interactions with member states.

The primary objectives of this study are:

1. To identify China's strategic interests and priorities within the SCO;
2. To assess the impact of Chinese economic policy on SCO projects;
3. To analyze multilateral cooperation dynamics under China's influence;
4. To examine problems and challenges faced by the SCO, as well as, Chinese approaches to resolving them;
5. To forecast the SCO's trajectory amid global geopolitical changes and China's leadership role.

The significance of this study lies in its systematic analysis of one of the most important regional organizations through the lens of Chinese influence. Its findings can inform policy recommendations for SCO member states, guide the strategic direction of the Organization, and serve as analytical tools for further academic inquiry into regional integration and multilateral diplomacy.

Results and Discussion

China's Strategic Interests and Priorities

China views the SCO as a mechanism for securing its western borders, promoting the Belt and Road Initiative, combating terrorism, separatism, and extremism, strengthening cultural diplomacy through educational and soft-power initiatives, advancing environmental sustainability, and promoting technological leadership. The SCO thus serves China's dual objectives: ensuring domestic stability while projecting international influence through a multipolar order.

Chinese Economic Policy and SCO Projects

China's BRI, supported by the AIIB and Silk Road Fund, has been central to financing infrastructure projects, roads, railways, pipelines, and digital corridors. These investments strengthen intra-SCO trade, improve energy security, and promote technological integration. Initiatives such as the Digital Silk Road illustrate China's ambition to dominate digital infrastructure and e-commerce within the bloc.

Trends in Multilateral Cooperation under China's Influence

China's leadership fosters expansion of transport and energy networks, deepened counterterrorism cooperation, enhanced cultural and humanitarian exchanges, promotion of digitalization, and strengthening of institutional mechanisms. These initiatives position the SCO as both a security alliance and a development platform.

Challenges and China's Approach

Challenges include divergent member interests, geopolitical rivalries, security threats, economic disparities, and territorial disputes. China addresses these through consensus-building, bilateral partnerships, investment funds, mediation, and expanding SCO dialogue with global institutions. A SWOT analysis highlights both opportunities, economic integration, security cooperation, global influence and threats such as external pressures, debt-trap criticisms, and internal fragmentation.

Future Scenarios for the SCO

Three scenarios emerge:

1. Consolidation deeper integration and stronger Chinese mediation, elevating the SCO as a global bloc.
2. Internal Fragmentation slowed Chinese growth and disputes weaken cohesion.
3. Adaptive flexibility reforms balance member interests and preserve multipolarity.

Conclusion

Thus the study has provided a comprehensive assessment of China's role in shaping the SCO. China's strategic vision, spanning economic integration, security cooperation, technological advancement, and cultural diplomacy, defines much of the Organization's trajectory.

While the SCO faces internal disagreements and external pressures, Chinese initiatives provide mechanisms for stability and growth. Scenario analysis highlights possible futures ranging from deeper consolidation to adaptive restructuring. Ultimately, the SCO's effectiveness will depend on balancing China's leadership with genuine multilateralism. China will remain central to the SCO's evolution, but its long-term success hinges on collective engagement and equitable cooperation among all members.

REFERENCES

Amrebaev, A. (2023). Novye obrazy ShOS v uslovijah menjajushhegosja mirovogo porjadka [New images of the SCO in a changing world order]. Retrieved from Zakon.kz. 05.07.2023 – URL:https://www.zakon.kz/mnenie/6399060-novye-obrazy-shos-v-usloviyakh-menyayushchegosya-mirovogo-poryadka.html (In Russian).

Chao, W. C. (2022). The political economy of China's rising role in the Shanghai Cooperation Organization (SCO): Leading with balance. The Chinese Economy, Vol. 55, No. 4, 293-302.

Dadabaev, T. (2014). Shanghai Cooperation Organization (SCO) regional identity formation from the perspective of the Central Asia States. Journal of Contemporary China, Vol. 23, No. 85, 102-118.

Fredholm, M. (2013). Understanding China's Policy and Intentions Towards the SCO. Himalayan and Central Asian Studies, Vol. 17, No. 3-4, 38-60.

Ho, D. (2022). Nacional'nye interesy Kitaja i Rossii v ramkah ShOS [National interests of China and Russia within the SCO]. Vestnik Moskovskogo gosudarstvennogo oblastnogo universiteti, No. 3, 88-99.

Kalandarshoev, G. A. (2020). Rol' i mesto Shanhajskoj organizacii sotrudnichestva v sisteme mezhdunarodnyh otnoshenij [The role and place of the Shanghai Cooperation Organization in the system of international relations], Molodoj uchjonyj, No. 48 (338), 108-110 (In Russian).

Kulincev, Ju. V. (2023). Prioritety Kitaja v ShOS v 2022 godu [China's priorities in the SCO in 2022]. Kitajskaja Narodnaja Respublika: politika, jekonomika, kul'tura 2022 [People's Republic of China: politics, economics, culture 2022]. M.: Institut Kitaja i sovremennoj Azii Rossijskoj akademii nauk, P. 319-328 (In Russian).

Kurylev, K. P., Barannik M. A., Stanis D. V. (2020). ShOS kak nesushhij jelement konstrukcii Bol'shoj Evrazii [SCO as a bearing element of the Greater Eurasia structure]. Postsovetskie issledovanija, Vol. 3. No. 8, 627-632 (In Russian).

Kushkumbaev, S.K. (2022). Kazahstan i Central'naja Azija mezhdu vyzovami iz proshlogo i grjadushhego. Sbornik statej, vystuplenij i interv'ju [Kazakhstan and Central Asia between challenges from the past and the future. Collection of articles, speeches, and interviews. Astana. 372 p. (In Russian).

Larin, V. (2016). Rossijsko-kitajskoe transgranich'e v kontekste proektov evrazijskoj integracii. Mirovaja jekonomika i mezh-dunarodnye otnoshenija [The Russian-Chinese cross-border area in the context of Eurasian integration projects]. World economy and international relations, No. 12, 69-81 (In Russian).

Lezheng, Zh. (2021). Rol' Kitaja v sozdanii i dejatel'nosti Shanhajskoj organizacii sotrudnichestva (2001–2012 gg.) [China's role in the establishment and operation of the Shanghai Cooperation Organization]. EAJeS i ShOS: po puti vzaimovygodnogo sotrudnichestva: materialy mezhdunar. kruglogo stola po innovacijam v mezhdunar. issled., Minsk, April 20. 2021 g. / O. N. Leshenjuk (gl. red.)]. [EAEU and SCO: along the path of mutually beneficial cooperation: materials of international. Round table on innovation in international. Research, Minsk, April 20. 2021 / Ed.: O. N. Leshenyuk. Minsk, Belarus. State University, 62-67 (In Russian).

Mamakhatov, T., Mallah, M. J. (2021). The role of the SCO countries in ensuring China's energy security. RUDN Journal of Economics, 29(4), 653–663.

Popović, S. (2018). The Role of the Shanghai Cooperation Organization in China's New Security Concept. Asian Issues, Vol. 4, No. 1, 73-100.

Rab, A., Zhilong, H. (2019). China and Shanghai Cooperation Organization (SCO): Belt and Road Initiative (BRI) perspectives. International Journal of Humanities and Social Sciences. Vol. 9, No. 2, 166-171.

Yuan, J. D. (2010). China plays a significant role in establishing and building the Shanghai Cooperation Organization (SCO). Journal of Contemporary China, Vol. 19, No. 67, 855-869.

7

Prospects for the Formation of a Central Asian Union: Implications for Regionalism

Aygerim Temirbaeva

ABSTRACT

This chapter examines the feasibility of establishing a Central Asian Union (CAU) and its potential influence on regionalism in Central Asia. The region, comprising Kazakhstan, Uzbekistan, Turkmenistan, Kyrgyzstan, and Tajikistan, has historically been shaped by complex political, economic, and cultural linkages that both facilitate and impede integration processes. In light of global challenges, such as shifting geopolitical dynamics, financial instability, and environmental crises, the idea of creating a CAU gains significance as a mechanism to reinforce regional cooperation and sustainability. The study analyzes the prerequisites for the formation of a CAU, including shared historical roots, geographical proximity, and common socio-economic challenges such as water management, energy security, and transportation infrastructure development. Particular attention is given to the role of existing regional organizations such as the Shanghai Cooperation Organization (SCO) and the Eurasian Economic Union (EAEU). The chapter concludes that the establishment of a CAU is feasible through a gradual, step-by-step approach beginning with economic integration, but requires strong political will from the region's leaders. The success of the CAU will ultimately depend on the ability of the Central Asian states to overcome internal differences and formulate a common strategy that can, over time, reinforce regionalism and make Central Asia more stable and independent.

Keywords: *Central Asian Union, regionalism, integration, cooperation, security.*

Introduction

Central Asia, located at the crossroads of Eurasia, occupies a distinctive position on the global stage owing to its strategic geography and abundant resource potential. Following the dissolution of the Soviet Union in 1991, five states, Kazakhstan, Kyrgyzstan, Tajikistan, Turkmenistan, and Uzbekistan, embarked on the path of independence, each confronted with the task of constructing its own development model. Against the backdrop of globalization, intensifying transnational threats, and heightened competition for resources, the notion of integration under a Central Asian Union has become increasingly relevant.

The significance of this study lies not only in the potential benefits of cooperation, such as economic growth and enhanced security, but also in the challenges stemming from divergent political systems, conflicting national interests, and the influence of external actors.

Geopolitically, Central Asia serves as a vital bridge between East and West, linking Europe, Russia, China, and South Asia. Its strategic importance is reinforced by major transport corridors, including China's "One Belt, One Road" initiative, as well as, access to the Caspian Sea and vast hydrocarbon resources. Economically, the region possesses considerable potential in trade, agriculture, and industry. However, fragmentation and weak infrastructure continue to limit this potential. A Central Asian Union could help dismantle trade barriers, harmonize water and energy management, and attract foreign investment. This raises a crucial question: how realistic is such integration, and how regionalism might shape its trajectory?

The purpose of this study is to assess the prospects for creating a Central Asian Union and to evaluate the role of regionalism as a driving force in this process. Specific objectives include exploring the historical context of integration and examining the political and economic factors shaping cooperation. Methodologically, the study employs qualitative analysis based on a review of scholarly literature, official documents, and speeches by regional leaders. Both primary sources (e.g., official statements) and secondary sources (e.g., academic works, analytical reports) are utilized.

The Concept of Regionalism in the Global Context

Regionalism in international relations refers to processes of cooperation and integration among states within a specific geographic region to achieve shared objectives economic, political, or cultural. The term gained prominence in the twentieth century, when globalization and rising interdependence prompted states to seek new forms of collaboration. Bjorn Hettne defines regionalism as "a multidimensional process involving not only economic cooperation but also the creation of a collective identity based on shared values and interests" [1].

History of Integration Processes in Central Asia

Following the collapse of the Soviet Union in 1991, the newly independent Central Asian republics inherited a legacy of deep interconnectedness shared infrastructure, centralized resource management, and a unifying ideology. With independence, however, these links dissolved, and each state sought to establish its own identity and economic system.

Economic and Social Factors: Opportunities and Obstacles

Central Asia's economic integration potentially rests on vast natural resources. Kazakhstan leads in oil and gas, Uzbekistan in gold and uranium, Turkmenistan in natural gas, while Kyrgyzstan and Tajikistan possess immense hydropower capacity. Despite this complementarity, unresolved disputes, particularly over water and energy resources, remain major barriers.

Security Threats

The region faces multidimensional security threats: terrorism, extremism, separatism, drug trafficking, and arms smuggling, exacerbated by instability in Afghanistan.

Positive Impacts of Regionalism

Regionalism can yield three major benefits for Central Asia: economic cooperation, strengthened security, and enhanced stability.

Conclusion

At present, the Central Asian Union remains more of an aspiration than a reality. Pragmatic, incremental steps in economic, environmental, and security cooperation are more likely in the near term. Future regionalism will likely evolve into a model of "soft regionalism", prioritizing functional cooperation while balancing national sovereignty with collective goals.

REFERENCES

1. Hettne B. Beyond the "new" regionalism // New Political Economy. - 2005. - Vol. 10(4).
2. Назарбаев за Центрально-Азиатский Союз. Электронный доступ. URL: https://iwpr.net/ru/global-voices/nazarbaev-za-centralno-aziatskiy-soyuz. (дата обращения: 24.03.2025).
3. Первая консультативная встреча глав государств Центральной Азии. Электронный ресурс. URL: https://uza.uz/ru/posts/pervaya-konsultativnaya-vstrecha-glav-gosudarstv-tsentralnoy-15-03-2018. (дата обращения: 22.03.2025).
4. Саммит глав государств Центральной Азии в Ташкенте придаст новый импульс региональной интеграции. Электронный ресурс. URL: https://www.newscentral asia.net/2019/12/02/central-asia-summit-tashkent-ru/. (дата обращения: 22.03.2025).
5. В Туркменистане прошла третья консультативная встреча президентов стран Центральной Азии. Электронный ресурс. URL: https://www.trta vaz.com.tr/ haber/rus/avrasyadan/v-turkmenistane-proshla-tretya-konsultativ naya-vstrecha-prezidentov-stran-tsen/610d322601a30a1c28ae1434. (дата обращения: 22.03.2025).
6. Президент Узбекистана выступил за повышение эффективности многостороннего сотрудничества в регионе. Электронный ресурс. URL: https://president.uz/ru/lists/view/5357. (дата обращения: 22.03.2025).
7. В Душанбе прошла Пятая консультативная встреча глав государств Центральной Азии. Электронный ресурс. URL: https://cis.minsk.by/ news/26058/v_ dushanbe_proshla_pjataja_konsultativnaja_vstrecha_glav_gosudarstv_central noj_azii (дата обращения: 22.03.2025).
8. Крупнейшие месторождения Казахстана. Электронный ресурс. URL: https://dprom.kz/dobycha/krupnejshie-mestorozhdeniya-kazahstana/ (дата обращения: 21.03.2025).
9. Природные ресурсы. Электронный ресурс. URL: https://dev-portal.miit.uz/ru/why-uzbekistan/natural-resources (дата обращения: 21.03.2025).
10. В шести областях Узбекистана нашли новые месторождения урана. Электронный ресурс. URL: https://tass.ru/ekonomika/21799409 (дата обращения: 21.03.2025).
11. Энергетическая политика Туркменистана: важность и перспективы газопровода ТАПИ. Электронный ресурс. URL: https://www.eurasian-research.org/publica tion/energy-policies-of-turkmenistan-importance-and-perspectives-of-tapi-natural-gas-pipeline/. (дата обращения: 21.03.2025).
12. О Кыргызской Республике. Электронный ресурс. URL: https://invest. gov.kg/ru/. (дата обращения: 21.03.2025).
13. Гидроэнергетические ресурсы Таджикистана. Электронный ресурс. URL: https://www.mewr.tj/?page_id=614#:~:text=%. (дата обращения: 21.03. 2025).

14. Маркова Е.А. Энергетическая политика стран Центральной Азии: основные итоги. Проблемы постсоветского пространства. 2020;7(3):365-372. https://doi.org/10.24 975/2313-8920-2020-7-3-365-372).
15. Торгово-экономическое сотрудничество стран Центральной Азии. Электронный ресурс. URL: https://www.cer.uz/en/post/publication/torgovo-ekonomiceskoe-sotrudnicestvo-stran-centralnoj-azii-v-period-pandemii. (дата обращения: 22.03.2025).

SECTION II

Security Challenges within the Regionalism Framework

8

Security Challenges in India and Its Neighbours: Traditional and Non-Traditional Threats

Jagatbir Singh

ABSTRACT

The concept of national security has expanded far beyond its traditional military framework to include economic, political, cyber, and environmental dimensions. Today, India faces both conventional threats, such as territorial disputes with Pakistan and China, and non-traditional challenges, including cyber warfare, climate change, and technological disruptions. As a major democracy and a rising power, India must address complex geopolitical and transnational threats. Internal vulnerabilities, particularly terrorism and insurgency, exacerbate its security concerns. This chapter explores the multifaceted nature of India's security challenges in the South Asian region and underscores the necessity of adopting a comprehensive, adaptive, and multidimensional approach to national security.

Keywords: *National Security, India's Security Challenges, Geopolitical Threats, Traditional and Non-Traditional Security, South Asian Security, China–India Conflict, Pakistan–India Relations, Terrorism and Insurgency in India, Cybersecurity, Technological Threats*

Introduction

For most, national security has traditionally been equated with military power, capability, and readiness. However, defining national security solely in the context of conventional warfare has become obsolete. In the contemporary era, the domain of security encompasses economic security, political security, energy security, homeland security, cybersecurity, human security, and environmental security, among others.

Today, national security extends beyond traditional territorial threats and hard power to include soft power, climate change, ransomware, critical minerals, artificial intelligence, and social media. Economic globalization and rapid technological transformations have multiplied unconventional threats. While new challenges continuously emerge, older threats remain unresolved, thereby expanding rather than contracting the scope of security concerns. India's unresolved territorial disputes resemble dormant volcanoes, unpredictable in their eruption, and demand constant attention and resources.

As one of the largest democracies and fastest-growing economies, India stands at a pivotal juncture in its pursuit of security. Its environment is defined by a complex interplay of traditional and transnational challenges. The country must defend both land and maritime borders against diverse and overlapping threats. Regional dynamics, economic constraints, technological advancements, and evolving geopolitical realities demand a comprehensive and multidimensional approach to ensure India's long-term security and prosperity.

Since independence, India has faced a fraught security environment. To the northwest, Pakistan's revisionist policies have resulted in wars and frequent skirmishes, with the Kashmir dispute remaining a central issue. In 1962, India fought a war with China, and the unresolved border disputes continue to cast a shadow, most recently visible in the Galwan clash of May 2020. Both China and Pakistan are nuclear-armed states, heightening the complexity of India's security calculus.

India also continues to grapple with the legacy of contested boundaries left by the colonial era, such as the Radcliffe Line, Johnson Line, McMahon Line, Line of Control, and Line of Actual Control. These unresolved territorial disputes with Pakistan and China obstruct cooperative regional security approaches. Internally, terrorism and insurgency constitute India's most pressing challenges. This chapter provides an overview of the broad spectrum of security threats confronting India, with a specific focus on the South Asian region.

The Evolving Geopolitical Scenario

The contemporary world is undergoing a transition toward multipolarity, in which India, supported by strong military capabilities and growing economic and diplomatic influence, has emerged as an essential actor. However, the strategic environment in which India pursues its security interests is characterized by volatility, uncertainty, complexity, and ambiguity (VUCA). The past decade has witnessed extraordinary geopolitical upheavals and a resurgence of great power competition. This period has also been defined by a troubling persistence of conflict.

Five strategic shocks, the COVID-19 pandemic, the Galwan standoff, the U.S. withdrawal from Afghanistan, the Ukraine War, and the Gaza Conflict, have significantly shaped global contestation in the post-Cold War order and directly affected India. Historical animosities, conflicting national interests, volatile flashpoints, dangerous military posturing, and a weakening United Nations Security Council (UNSC) have all contributed to escalating risks to international peace.

Wars in Ukraine and Gaza illustrate the changing nature of warfare, where the line between declared and undeclared wars has blurred. Niche and disruptive technologies act as catalysts for asymmetric warfare, altering deterrence and the use of force. Swarm drones and missile attacks, demonstrated by Iran and its proxies, epitomize these shifts. Regional conflicts in West Asia have pitted Israel and the United States against Iran and its allies, destabilizing the region further. The Gaza conflict has plunged West Asia into a deep humanitarian and geopolitical crisis. India has adopted a nuanced position, condemning Hamas' terrorist attacks while supporting a two-state solution and avoiding commitment to divisive UN resolutions.

Elsewhere, geopolitical turbulence continues. The Trump administration pressured allies to increase defense budgets, triggering shifts in military postures in regions such as the Baltics, the South China Sea, and the Taiwan Strait. The abrogation of nuclear arms-control treaties has reintroduced destabilizing dynamics into global strategy, illustrated by Pakistan's doctrine of full-spectrum nuclear deterrence. Meanwhile, the Indo-Pacific has emerged as the primary theatre of great power rivalry. The central question remains whether China can become Asia's dominant power, thereby displacing the United States. Washington's vision of a "Free and Open Indo-Pacific," finds resonance in the strategies of Japan and certain European states, reinforced by U.S. treaty alliances.

Russia, since 2014, has pursued a "Pivot to Asia" policy, strengthening trade with Asian economies, especially China. Key aspects include the development of Russia's Far East, the Northern Sea Route, and major energy corridors such as the second Trans-Siberian pipeline to China. India's strategic connectivity is linked through projects like the International North–South Transport Corridor (INSTC) and the Vladivostok–Chennai transit corridor. These developments highlight the complexity of India's evolving geopolitical environment, which demands nuanced understanding and robust strategic responses.

India's Traditional Security Threats

India's relations with its neighbours are defined by a complex interplay of cooperation and competition, shaped by political alignments, strategic opportunities, and security challenges.

China

Despite brief episodes of cooperation epitomised by the "Hindi-Chini Bhai Bhai" sentiment, China has remained a major security concern for Indian policymakers. The central irritant has been the boundary demarcation issue. When India attained independence, it assumed that the McMahon Line would be recognised as the international border. However, the People's Republic of China rejected it, branding it a colonial construct. This led to the 1962 Sino-Indian War, during which China occupied thousands of square kilometres of Indian territory in Aksai Chin and near the McMahon Line. Pakistan's ceding of territory in 1963 further deepened the deadlock. Although relations revived in 1976, the border dispute remains unresolved. Despite cooperation in some areas, boundary negotiations have produced no breakthrough. Complicating matters are China's support to Pakistan, its assertive role in the South China Sea, and the China–Pakistan Economic Corridor (CPEC). Relations worsened after the

Doklam standoff in 2017 and the Galwan clash in 2020. The military capacity gap between the two remains substantial, particularly in advanced technologies.

Pakistan

Since its creation, Pakistan has remained a central factor in India's security calculus. India has fought four wars with Pakistan, while the Kashmir dispute persists as a perpetual irritant. Additional disputes, including Sir Creek, Tulbul, and Siachen, have strained relations. Despite the expectation that nuclearisation might stabilise relations, Pakistan continued its revisionist policies. Post-1989, it intensified its proxy war strategy by supporting terrorism. Even amid domestic instability, Pakistan allocates disproportionate resources to military modernisation. The deepening strategic partnership between Pakistan and China adds a collusive threat. The China–Pakistan axis, born in 1962, has matured into an "all-weather" partnership, resilient even to global shifts.

Nepal

Nepal's geographic location makes it strategically vital. Strains emerged after Kathmandu's 2020 map dispute and growing Chinese influence. The porous border enables smuggling and militant movements, posing direct threats to India.

Bhutan

India and Bhutan share exemplary relations, with Bhutan acting as a buffer against China. However, Beijing's pressure on Thimphu and the Doklam dispute raise concerns about India's Siliguri Corridor security.

Myanmar

India and Myanmar share deep-rooted ties and a long border. However, insurgency, arms smuggling, and the post-coup civil war complicate security. Refugee flows, especially Rohingya, add to the challenges.

Bangladesh

Bangladesh shares the longest land border with India. Political turbulence, the rise of Islamist forces, and growing Chinese influence complicate relations, alongside unresolved cross-border issues.

Sri Lanka

Sri Lanka's strategic location makes it a site of India-China competition. Indian aid helped during its economic crisis, but political shifts could tilt Colombo towards Beijing. Tamil grievances remain unresolved.

Maldives

The Maldives holds strategic significance in the Arabian Sea. Despite India's assistance, pro-China political currents and the "India Out" campaign complicate bilateral ties, though goodwill among citizens offers hope.

The Indian Ocean Region (IOR) and India's Neighbours

The Indian Ocean has become central to India's security, with most trade and energy supplies passing through its waters. The IOR-ARC has facilitated cooperation. However, China's Belt and Road Initiative, its dual-use infrastructure projects, and competition in the Indo-Pacific challenge India's maritime strategy. India has responded by strengthening QUAD and naval cooperation with other major powers.

India's Internal Security Challenges

India faces internal threats closely tied to external influences. Pakistan-backed terrorism in Kashmir has expanded beyond the valley, targeting major cities. Left-Wing Extremism continues to affect central states, exploiting tribal populations. Northeastern insurgencies, fuelled by ethnic tensions and cross-border sanctuaries, persist. Illegal migration from Bangladesh has added demographic pressures, while ethnic conflicts in Manipur and unresolved Naga issues undermine stability.

India's Non-Traditional Threats

India also grapples with non-traditional threats including cyber warfare, climate change, pandemics, and technological disruptions. Cyberattacks have targeted institutions and infrastructure. Climate change threatens food and water security, with Himalayan glacier melt endangering river systems. These transnational issues demand cooperative, multidimensional responses.

India and the Central Asian Republics

Central Asia offers strategic opportunities for India as a gateway to Eurasia and a source of energy. Shared concerns about extremism and Afghanistan drive cooperation. India has engaged through initiatives like the International North–South Transport Corridor and joint security dialogues. However, limited connectivity and China's strong presence constrain India's influence.

India's Strategies for National Security

India's security strategies emphasise defence modernisation, diversification of partnerships, regional cooperation, and the strengthening of cyber and energy security. Its Act East Policy, Indo-Pacific outreach, and deepened ties with the QUAD highlight proactive measures. Simultaneously, counterterrorism, insurgency management, and economic resilience remain core priorities.

Conclusion

India's security landscape is characterised by both traditional and non-traditional threats, shaped by its geography, neighbours, and global shifts. The challenges of terrorism, insurgency, border disputes, and great power competition converge with climate, cyber, and economic insecurities. Navigating these requires a comprehensive, adaptive, and multidimensional approach. India's ability to ensure long-term stability and prosperity will depend on its capacity to balance external pressures, manage internal vulnerabilities, and leverage its democratic and economic strengths in a multipolar world.

REFERENCES

ANI. (2021, January 12). Increase in cooperation between China and Pak in both military and non-military sectors: Army Chief. The Economic Times. https://economic times.indiatimes.com/news/defence/increase-in-cooperation-between-china-pak-in-both-military-non-military-sectors-army-chief/videoshow/80232805.cms

Asia-Pacific Center For Security Studies. (2010). Issues for engagement: Asian perspectives on transnational security challenges. Asia-Pacific Center For Security Studies.

Chaudhuri, S. (2024). Non-Traditional Security. Globalindiafoundation.org. https://global indiafoundation.org/nontraditionalsecurity.html

Drezner, D. W. (2024, August 12). How Everything Became National Security. Foreign Affairs. https://web.archive.org/web/20250224141458/https://www.foreignaffairs.com/united-states/how-everything-became-national-security-drezner

Gafoor, A. (2017). The Kashmir dispute, 1947-2012. Tulika Books.

George, A. A. (2019, March 6). Kashmir Issue - Understand the multiple dimensions. ClearIAS. https://www.clearias.com/kashmir-issue/

Ghosh, S. (2024a, September 24). Sri Lanka: How Anura Dissanayake's presidency will test India's diplomatic agility. Firstpost. https://www.firstpost.com/opinion/sri-lanka-how-anura-dissanayakes-presidency-will-test-indias-diplomatic-agility-13818519.html

Ghosh, S. (2024b, September 26). Opinion | Sri Lanka Gets A New President: Decoding Key Challenges for India. News18. https://www.news18.com/opinion/opinion-sri-lanka-gets-a-new-president-decoding-key-challenges-for-india-9064828.html

Harsh, V. (2025, March 23). How better India-China ties are a greater necessity than a choice. Firstpost. https://www.firstpost.com/world/how-better-india-china-ties-are-a-greater-necessity-than-a-choice-13873720.html

Kumar, A. (2012). The Terror Challenge in South Asia and the Prospect of Regional Cooperation. Institute For Defence Studies & Analyses.

Longley, R. (2021, September 24). National Security Definition and Examples. ThoughtCo. https://www.thoughtco.com/national-security-definition-and-examples-5197450

Menon, S. (n.d.). India's National Security: Challenges and Issues. Journal of Air Power & Space Studies, Vol. 7(Journal No. 2 SUMMER 2012 (April-June)). Retrieved March 21, 2025, from https://capsindia.org/wp-content/uploads/2022/09/Shivshankar-Menon.pdf

Menon, S. S., & Select any. (2012, April 6). 'External environment doesn't support India's transformation'. The Indian Express. https://indianexpress.com/article/opinion/ columns/external-environment-doesn-t-support-india/

Moorthy, N. S. (2025, January 24). Maldives and India: Navigating strengthened ties amid geopolitical shifts. Orfonline.org; Observer Research Foundation. https://www.orfonline.org/expert-speak/maldives-and-india-navigating-strengthened-ties-amid-geopolitical-shifts

Riedel, B. (2015). JFK's Forgotten Crisis. Brookings Institution Press.

Ritika V Kapoor. (2020, April 9). Significance of Maldives to India. National Maritime Foundation. https://maritimeindia.org/significance-of-the-maldives-to-india/

Sharma, L. (2022, February 18). India - Myanmar relations | Timeline. Free UPSC IAS Preparation Syllabus and Materials for Aspirants. https://forumias.com/blog/india-myanmar-relations-timeline/

Shivane, A. B. (2023, December 9). National Security in the 21st Century: Challenges and Strategies. Defence Research and Studies. https://dras.in/national-security-in-21st-century-challenges-and-strategies/

Singh, M. G. V. K. (2025, January 11). How China is damming rivers in Tibet to build "liquid bomb" against India. Firstpost. https://www.firstpost.com/opinion/how-china-is-damming-rivers-in-tibet-to-build-liquid-bomb-against-india-13851802.html

Singh, M. G. J. (2023, July 29). How Pakistan is preparing a nuclear umbrella to foster terrorism against India. Firstpost. https://www.firstpost.com/opinion/how-pakistan-is-preparing-nuclear-umbrella-to-foster-terrorism-against-india-12933242.html

Singh, M. G. V., & Singh, M. G. J. (2021). The China-Pakistan Collusive Threat, USI Occasional Papers, 3. http://www.usiofindia.org/publications.php?filter=topic&query =collusive

VisionIAS. (2025, January 21). India-Bhutan relations I Current Affairs I Vision IAS. Current Affairs I Vision IAS. https://dce.visionias.in/monthly-magazine/2025-01-22/inter national-relations/india-bhutan-relations-1

What's happening in Myanmar? I Start Here. (2025). Al Jazeera. https://www.aljazeera.com/program/start-here/2025/1/31/whats-happening-in-myanmar-start-here-2

Yadav, R. S. (n.d.). India's Security Concerns – Foreign Policy of India. Ebooks.in flibnet. ac.in. https://ebooks.inflibnet.ac.in/psp06/chapter/indias-security-concerns/

9

Environmental Security in Central Asia

Shakhrozoda Anvarovna

ABSTRACT

Environmental security in Central Asia is shaped by a complex interplay of natural, anthropogenic, and institutional factors. This chapter examines the region's principal environmental challenges, including the desiccation of the Aral Sea, desertification, pollution, biodiversity loss, and radioactive contamination. By integrating geographical, political, and economic perspectives, it highlights obstacles to sustainable development. Historically, Soviet-era industrialization and irrigation projects, notably forced collectivization and the expansion of cotton monoculture, resulted in excessive water withdrawals and severe ecosystem degradation. In the post-Soviet era, weak environmental regulations and the absence of effective transboundary water governance have further aggravated ecological issues. Regional fragmentation and political competition between upstream and downstream states have hindered the adoption of coordinated ecological strategies. Climate change compounds these challenges, threatening ecosystems across the region. The retreat of the Tien Shan and Pamir glaciers, sources of up to 70% of Central Asia's river flow has placed water security at risk. Increasing droughts, floods, and extreme weather events are reducing agricultural productivity and worsening living conditions. According to WHO data, rising levels of pollution are directly correlated with increases in respiratory and infectious diseases.

The study outlines three possible scenarios:

1. *Optimistic Scenario: International cooperation and the expansion of renewable energy (30% of the energy mix by 2050) drive improvements.*
2. *Pessimistic Scenario: Continued inaction worsens environmental and social instability.*
3. *Realistic Scenario: Moderate progress in Kazakhstan and Uzbekistan is achieved, but without broader regional cohesion.*

Keywords: *Environmental security, Central Asia, water resources, political stability, regional cooperation, climate change, sustainable development.*

Introduction

Central Asia is a vast landlocked region located in the heart of the Eurasian continent, encompassing five sovereign states: Kazakhstan, Kyrgyzstan, Tajikistan, Turkmenistan, and Uzbekistan (Центральная Азия//Большая российская энциклопедия. URL: https://bigenc.ru/c/tsentral-naia-aziia-ef669e). Covering nearly 4 million square kilometres, it ranks among the largest continental areas in the world. The region's environment is highly diverse, featuring steppe landscapes, deserts, mountain ranges, and rare oasis ecosystems. Its most significant geomorphological features include the Karakum and Kyzyl-Kum deserts, the Tien Shan and Pamir mountain ranges, and major hydrological systems such as the Amu Darya River basin and the Aral Sea, once a vast inland water body but now severely degraded.

The climate of Central Asia is shaped by its extreme continental character, determined by its distance from oceans and the presence of orographic barriers that block the inflow of moist air masses. Seasonal variations are stark, with summer temperatures reaching +40°C and winter temperatures dropping to –30°C (Центральная Азия: География, Климат и Культура // Бегемот. URL: https://begemot.ai/projects/2007169-centralnaia-aziia-geografiia-klimat-i-kultura). Precipitation patterns also vary dramatically from less than 100–200 mm annually in arid deserts to over 1,000 mm in mountainous zones. These climatic and geographical conditions have historically shaped the region's ecological systems, favoring nomadic pastoralism while limiting irrigated agriculture to small oasis zones.

From the perspective of climatic zonation, Central Asia is divided into distinct regions, each exerting unique environmental pressures. In the north, Kazakhstan's steppe ecosystems, with moderate precipitation of 300-400 mm annually, are prone to soil erosion and desertification caused by intensive grazing and unsustainable agricultural practices. Further south, in Turkmenistan and Uzbekistan, desert and semi-desert landscapes dominate. These areas, characterized by minimal precipitation and high evaporation, are particularly vulnerable to soil salinization and vegetation decline. By contrast, the mountainous regions of Kyrgyzstan and Tajikistan belong to the alpine zone, with cooler and more humid conditions. These upland areas are crucial for regional hydrology, as glacial meltwater from the Tien Shan and Pamir ranges sustains the Syr Darya and Amu Darya rivers. Yet, excessive water withdrawals for irrigation in downstream lowlands have contributed to severe ecological consequences, most notably the desiccation of the Aral Sea.

Thus, the region's environmental degradation arises from the combined impact of natural factors such as aridity, extreme temperature variations, and glacial retreat, and anthropogenic pressures, including over-extraction of water resources, intensive monoculture farming, and chemical pollution.

Historical Roots of Environmental Degradation

The roots of Central Asia's current environmental crises lie in Soviet-era policies that prioritized economic output over ecological sustainability. Beginning in the 1930s, Stalin's industrialization and collectivization campaigns imposed centralized strategies that restructured the region's economy and environment. Cotton monoculture was expanded as a key pillar of the USSR's planned economy, transforming Central Asia into the empire's "cotton belt."

To sustain large-scale agricultural production, massive irrigation projects were constructed, most notably the Karakum Canal (1954–1988), which stretched over 1,300 kilometres. Irrigated areas in the Syr Darya and Amu Darya river basins expanded to 7.5 million hectares by the 1980s. While these measures boosted agricultural output, they led to excessive water withdrawals, which in turn caused the catastrophic shrinkage of the Aral Sea, once the world's fourth-largest inland water body. By the early 21st century, the sea had lost 90% of its surface area and 75% of its volume.

The ecological consequences were devastating:

1. Rising soil salinization reduced agricultural fertility.
2. The fishing industry, which had produced over 40,000 tons annually in the 1960s, collapsed.
3. Delta ecosystems degraded, and toxic dust storms carrying up to 75 million tons of salt annually spread across distances of up to 500 km. (Миклин, П. *Катастрофа Аральского моря* // Ежегодный обзор наук о Земле и планетах. 2007. Т. 35. С. 47–72.)

Soviet development was also marked by disregard for environmental oversight. Economic goals were consistently prioritized in five-year plans, with little concern for long-term ecosystem resilience. Simultaneously, Soviet nuclear and uranium programs left a lasting legacy of contamination. Between 1949 and 1989, 475 atomic tests were conducted at the Semipalatinsk Test Site, while extensive uranium extraction created more than 50 tailing sites across Kazakhstan, Kyrgyzstan, and Tajikistan, collectively storing approximately 800 million tons of radioactive waste.

These sites remain unstable, vulnerable to erosion, landslides, and seismic activity, leading to radioactive leaks into groundwater and river systems. As a result, radioactive contamination has become a transboundary threat, with long-term ecological and health consequences for the entire region. (МАГАТЭ. *Радиологические условия в районах, затронутых добычей и переработкой урана в Центральной Азии*. Вена: Международное агентство по атомной энергии, 2015. 89 с.)

Taken together, the Soviet legacy of forced monoculture, aggressive irrigation, and unchecked industrial and nuclear programs entrenched deep ecological vulnerabilities in Central Asia. These historical policies laid the foundation for the region's present environmental insecurity, magnified by weak post-Soviet institutions and accelerating climate change.

Post-Soviet Environmental Challenges

After the collapse of the Soviet Union, Central Asia inherited a fragile ecological system already weakened by decades of unsustainable practices. Instead of recovery, the post-Soviet period has seen the persistence, and in some cases intensification of environmental degradation due to weak institutions, economic dependence on resource-intensive sectors, and fragmented governance.

Agricultural Pressures and Water Overuse

Agriculture remains the dominant consumer of natural resources, particularly in Turkmenistan and Uzbekistan. Cotton farming alone accounts for up to 90% of water use, placing immense pressure on regional hydrological systems. The reliance on intensive irrigation continues to exacerbate soil salinization and land degradation. At the same time, large quantities of fertilizers and pesticides are applied, up to 200–300 kg/ha annually, leading to nitrate and phosphate contamination of water bodies. Concentrations in the Amu Darya and Syr Darya basins frequently exceed permissible levels by two to three times (ЕЭК ООН. *Вторая оценка трансграничных рек, озер и подземных вод*. Женева: ООН, 2011. 448 с.). This has accelerated eutrophication, reduced biodiversity, and undermined the self-purification capacity of rivers.

Industrial Development and Air Pollution

Industrialization, particularly in Kazakhstan, has perpetuated environmental stress. The energy sector remains dominated by coal, which supplies 70% of Kazakhstan's electricity. Metallurgical industries contribute additional pollution, releasing approximately 1.5 million tons of sulphur dioxide (SO_2) annually, along with nitrogen oxides and fine particulate matter. In industrial centres such as Almaty and Karaganda, particulate matter concentrations of 50–70 $\mu g/m^3$ exceed WHO standards by five to seven times. This poor air quality is directly correlated with a 20–30% rise in chronic respiratory illnesses over the past two decades (ВОЗ. *Загрязнение атмосферного воздуха: Глобальная оценка воздействия и бремени болезней.* Женева: Всемирная организация здравоохранения, 2016. – 121 с.).

Biodiversity Loss

Central Asia's biodiversity is increasingly under threat from both climate change and anthropogenic pressures. Ecosystem degradation in riparian forests and alpine meadows has placed endemic species such as the snow leopard (*Panthera uncia*) and the saiga antelope (*Saiga tatarica*) at critical risk. Habitat fragmentation, poaching, and climate-related habitat loss have compounded these threats. According to the International Union for Conservation of Nature (IUCN), more than 20% of the region's flora and fauna are classified as vulnerable or endangered (IUCN. *The IUCN Red List of Threatened Species*. Gland: IUCN, 2022, URL: https://www.iucnredlist.org).

Radioactive Waste Legacy

One of the most pressing inherited challenges is radioactive contamination from Soviet-era uranium mining and nuclear activities. Kyrgyzstan, Tajikistan, and Kazakhstan together host more than 50 uranium tailing storage sites containing an estimated 800 million tons of radioactive waste. The instability of these sites, particularly in seismically active areas, facilitates the migration of radionuclides such as uranium-238 and radium-226 into groundwater and rivers. This presents a long-term environmental and public health hazard across borders (IAEA. *Radiological Conditions in the Areas Affected by Uranium Mining and Milling in Central Asia*, Vienna: International Atomic Energy Agency, 2015. 89 p.).

Climate Change and Regional Vulnerabilities

Climate change is compounding Central Asia's environmental fragility, intensifying both natural and anthropogenic stresses. According to the Intergovernmental Panel on Climate Change (IPCC), the region's average annual temperature has risen by 1.5–2°C in recent decades, a rate that exceeds global averages (IPCC. *Climate Change 2021: The Physical Science Basis.* Cambridge: Cambridge University Press, 2021. p. 2391). This warming trend is accelerating the recession of the Tien Shan and Pamir glaciers, which serve as the primary reservoirs of freshwater for the Amu Darya and Syr Darya rivers. Projections indicate that by 2050, glacial volume could decline by 30–50% (Известия РАН. *Изменение климата на Тянь-Шане в голоцене.//Известия РАН. Серия географическая.* URL: https://izvestia.igras.ru/jour/article/download/342/335). This would severely undermine water security for millions of people in the region.

Intensification of Extreme Weather

Shifts in climate patterns are also increasing the frequency and severity of extreme meteorological events. Droughts in Turkmenistan and Uzbekistan's desert zones are exacerbating water scarcity, reducing agricultural yields, and intensifying food insecurity. Meanwhile, the accelerated melting of snow and glacial ice in the mountains has heightened the frequency of floods, which destroy infrastructure and pose direct risks to human safety.

Desertification is expanding at alarming rates. Rising temperatures and chronic water shortages have further reduced arable land, jeopardizing the long-term viability of agriculture. Over the past 30 years, desert zones have expanded by approximately 100,000 km², while 40% of arable land and 60% of pastures have been affected by salinization and degradation (ФАО. *Состояние земельных и водных ресурсов мира для продовольствия и сельского хозяйства.* Рим: FAO, 2021. – 394 с.).

Impacts on Biodiversity

Climate change is placing immense pressure on the region's biodiversity. Endemic and vulnerable species, such as the snow leopard (*Panthera uncia*) and riparian forest ecosystems, face increasing threats as ecological niches shift and habitats fragment. Expanding aridity and the collapse of alpine and riparian ecosystems are pushing over 20% of regional flora and fauna into vulnerable or endangered categories (IUCN. *Red List of Threatened Species.* Gland: IUCN, 2022. URL: https://www.iucnredlist.org).

Socio-Economic Consequences

The economic consequences of climate-driven environmental degradation are severe. Crop productivity is declining, particularly for staples such as cotton and wheat, undermining food security and increasing reliance on imports. In Uzbekistan, cotton yields have fallen by 25% since the 1990s, while Kazakhstan's wheat output has dropped by 15% due to frequent droughts lasting up to 20 days annually.

At the same time, rising temperatures and dust storms are contributing to deteriorating public health. WHO data show that air pollution levels in cities like Almaty and Karaganda exceed safe standards by five to seven times, correlating with a 20–30% increase in chronic respiratory illnesses (WHO. *Ambient Air Pollution: A Global Assessment of Exposure and Burden of Disease.* Geneva: World Health Organization, 2016.121 p.). Toxic dust storms from the desiccated Aral Sea, carrying up to 75 million tons of salt annually, have contributed to a 15% rise in lung cancer cases since the 1990s, while child mortality from related illnesses has risen by 10% in affected areas of Uzbekistan and Turkmenistan.

Water scarcity, exacerbated by the 10–15 km³ annual reduction in glacial runoff and irrigation inefficiencies, has further worsened living conditions. In rural Tajikistan and Kyrgyzstan, where less than 60% of the population has access to safe drinking water, nitrate and phosphate contamination of the Syr Darya and Amu Darya rivers has fuelled the spread of waterborne diseases such as hepatitis A and dysentery (ЕЭК ООН. *Вторая оценка трансграничных рек, озер и подземных вод*. Женева: ООН, 2011. 448 с.).

Socio-Economic and Political Implications

Environmental degradation in Central Asia has far-reaching consequences that extend beyond ecosystems, shaping public health, food security, social stability, and political dynamics. The interplay of ecological stress and weak governance makes the region particularly vulnerable to socio-economic and political disruption.

Public Health Crises

The deterioration of air, water, and soil quality has led to widespread health risks. Air pollution in industrial centres such as Almaty and Karaganda, where particulate matter levels exceed WHO standards by five to seven times, has been linked to a 20–30% rise in respiratory diseases, including asthma and chronic bronchitis, over the past two decades (ВОЗ. *Загрязнение атмосферного воздуха: Глобальная оценка воздействия и бремени болезней*. – Женева: Всемирная организация здравоохранения, 2016. 121 с.). Toxic dust storms from the dried Aral Sea basin, carrying up to 75 million tons of salt annually, have caused a 15% increase in lung cancer cases since the 1990s, alongside a 10% rise in child mortality in parts of Uzbekistan and Turkmenistan (Миклин, П. *Катастрофа Аральского моря // Ежегодный обзор наук о Земле и планетах*. 2007. Т. 35. С. 47–72).

Water scarcity and contamination further undermine public health. Nitrate and phosphate pollution of the Syr Darya and Amu Darya rivers, often exceeding permissible levels by 2–3 times, combined with declining glacial runoff, has fuelled the spread of gastrointestinal infections such as hepatitis A and dysentery. Rural communities in Tajikistan and Kyrgyzstan, where less than 60% of residents have access to safe drinking water, are most affected (ЕЭК ООН. *Вторая оценка трансграничных рек, озер и подземных вод*. Женева: ООН, 2011. 448 с.). These health crises strain fragile healthcare systems, increase public spending on health (up to 2% of GDP), and reduce labor productivity by 10–15%.

Food Security and Agricultural Decline

Agriculture, employing 60% of the population and forming the backbone of regional economies, is under severe pressure. Desertification affects 40% of arable land, while salinization has degraded 60% of pastures. Crop yields have declined sharply: Uzbekistan's cotton output has dropped by 25% since the 1990s, while Kazakhstan's wheat production has fallen by 15% due to recurrent droughts. Outdated irrigation systems, which lose up to 40% of water, further limit productivity, particularly in Turkmenistan, where agriculture depends heavily on the Karakum Canal.

As a result, the region, historically reliant on agriculture, now imports up to 20% of its grain, undermining food sovereignty and increasing vulnerability to global market fluctuations. The collapse of Aral Sea fisheries, from 40,000 tons annually in the 1960s to zero today has eliminated a vital food source for poor communities, deepening economic and nutritional insecurity.

Migration and Urban Strain

Declining agricultural productivity and deteriorating living conditions have fuelled migration. Since 2010, more than 2 million people have left rural areas of Uzbekistan and Tajikistan, moving to urban centers such as Tashkent and Dushanbe or emigrating abroad to Russia and Kazakhstan. Rapid urbanization has intensified pressure on infrastructure, leading to the expansion of informal settlements, rising unemployment, and growing social tensions (CABAR.asia.*Природные экосистемы стран Центральной Азии стремительно разрушаются* // https://cabar.asia/ru/ prirodnye-ekosistemy-stran-tsentralnoj-azii-stremitelno-razrushayutsya).

Resource Conflicts and Regional Fragmentation

Competition over scarce water resources has triggered recurrent disputes between upstream and downstream states. Tajikistan and Kyrgyzstan prioritize hydropower projects such as the Rogun Dam, while Uzbekistan and Turkmenistan depend on irrigation for agriculture. Since 2000, over 50 water-related conflicts have been recorded, including violent clashes in the Fergana Valley in 2016 and 2021 (Вегерих, К. *Гидрогегемония в бассейне Амударьи // Водная политика.* 2008. Т. 10, Доп. 2. С. 71–88). The inability of institutions such as the Interstate Commission for Water Coordination

(ICWC) to effectively regulate water distribution underscores the persistence of geopolitical competition, where natural resources serve as instruments of power.

Economic Costs

Environmental degradation has systemic economic consequences. Agricultural losses alone account for 3–5% of GDP annually. Kazakhstan's declining grain yields cost approximately $1.2 billion, while Uzbekistan's cotton deficit results in losses of $800 million. The costs of ecological mitigation are equally staggering: $10 billion is required for Aral Sea reclamation projects, while stabilization of uranium tailings demands an additional $1.5 billion, sums that exceed the fiscal capacity of low-income countries such as Tajikistan, where per capita GDP is only $1,200 (МАГАТЭ. *Радиологические условия.* Вена: МАГАТЭ, 2015, 89 с.).

Reliance on external aid from the World Bank, Asian Development Bank, and other donors has increased, deepening economic dependence and exposing the region to external market vulnerabilities. The combined impact of agricultural decline, rising healthcare costs, and climate adaptation burdens is contributing to economic stagnation and heightening the risk of social unrest.

National Strategies for Environmental Security

Central Asian states have adopted diverse environmental security strategies shaped by their political systems, economic capacities, and geopolitical priorities. While Kazakhstan and Uzbekistan have taken relatively proactive steps, Tajikistan and Kyrgyzstan remain constrained by poverty and weak institutions, and Turkmenistan continues to prioritize economic isolation and gas exports over ecological reform.

Kazakhstan

As the region's largest economy, with a GDP of approximately $200 billion, Kazakhstan has positioned itself as a leader in sustainable development through its "Green Economy" strategy (2013). Key goals include reducing GDP carbon intensity by 40% by 2050 and increasing the share of renewable energy sources (RES) to 50%. These measures are driven by the need to diversify an economy heavily reliant on hydrocarbons, which account for around 20% of GDP, and to strengthen the country's international reputation.

Despite ambitious targets, implementation remains weak. Environmental initiatives receive less than 1% of GDP in funding, while resistance from the energy lobby and insufficient inter-agency coordination hinder progress. By 2025, renewable energy accounted for only 10% of the national energy mix, falling short of strategic objectives (*Стратегия «Казахстан-2050»: Новый политический курс состоявшегося государства.* Астана: Правительство РК, 2013. 48 с.).

Uzbekistan

Uzbekistan has taken a pragmatic approach through its "Action Strategy for 2017–2021", which prioritizes modernizing irrigation infrastructure and reclaiming degraded lands around the Aral Sea. Pilot programs have reduced water losses from 40% to 25%, while large-scale sexual planting projects covering over 500,000 hectares, have helped stabilize soil and reduce toxic dust storms. These initiatives reflect President Shavkat Mirziyoyev's political commitment to addressing historical ecological debts and improving domestic living standards. However, widespread implementation is constrained by budgetary limitations, as the country's per capita GDP remains approximately $2,000. (*Стратегия действий по пяти приоритетным направлениям развития Республики Узбекистан в 2017–2021 годах.* Ташкент: Кабинет Министров РУ, 2017. 32 с.).

Tajikistan

Tajikistan's National Development Strategy 2030 emphasizes sustainable water management, consistent with its role as an upstream state in the Amu Darya basin and its reliance on hydropower, which supplies 90% of its electricity. However, chronic poverty (per capita GDP of $1,200), weak infrastructure, and pervasive corruption have hindered implementation. Flagship projects such as the Rogun Hydropower Plant remain stalled in prolonged construction phases, reflecting the country's limited capacity to transform strategic plans into practical results (*Национальная стратегия развития Республики Таджикистан до 2030 года.* – Душанбе: Правительство РТ, 2016. 96 с.).

Kyrgyzstan

Kyrgyzstan has prioritized radioactive waste management through its "Rehabilitation Program" (2018), focusing on uranium tailings, which present serious transboundary risks. However, the country's efforts are hampered by seismic activity, limited access to advanced technologies, and a high dependence on international donors. Without sustained external support, progress on stabilizing contaminated sites remains minimal (*Программа реабилитации территорий, пострадавших от урановых отходов.*Бишкек: Правительство КР, 2018. – 28 с.).

Turkmenistan

Turkmenistan has formally committed to ecological reform through its "National Strategy 2040", but real action is minimal. The country's closed authoritarian system prioritizes gas exports, which contribute 40% of GDP. However, the absence of international engagement prevents meaningful implementation. (*Национальная стратегия устойчивого развития Туркменистана до 2040 года.* Ашхабад: Правительство ТМ, 2020. 36 с.).

Comparative Analysis

Kazakhstan and Uzbekistan are the most proactive due to their stronger economies and relatively more open political environments. Tajikistan and Kyrgyzstan face severe structural constraints, while Turkmenistan's isolationist stance blocks substantive reforms. Overall, these disparities highlight the urgent need for regional coordination to address shared environmental challenges that transcend national borders.

International Cooperation

Given the limited financial and institutional capacities of Central Asian states, international cooperation plays a critical role in addressing environmental challenges. Global organizations, regional bodies, and non-governmental actors provide essential resources, expertise, and policy support, though their effectiveness often depends on the political will of national governments.

United Nations Agencies

The United Nations Development Programme (UNDP) and UN Environment Programme (UNEP) have invested more than $200 million since 2015 in Aral Sea restoration projects. Initiatives include planting 1.5 million hectares of saxaul on the dried seabed, which has reduced dust storms by 20% and promoted transnational cooperation in the Syr Darya basin (ПРООН. *Годовой отчет 2020: Центральная Азия.* Нью-Йорк: UNDP, 202, 68 с.)

The World Health Organization (WHO) has provided crucial data linking environmental degradation to public health outcomes, noting a 20–30% increase in respiratory diseases in Kazakhstan. This has driven domestic efforts to curb industrial emissions and reinforced international accountability in environmental health policy (ВОЗ, *Загрязнение атмосферного воздуха: Глобальная оценка воздействия и бремени болезней.* Женева: ВОЗ, 2016. 121 с.).

The Global Environment Facility (GEF) has allocated $50 million since 2010 to combat desertification, financing pasture and forest restoration across degraded lands in the Kyzylkum and Karakum deserts. These projects have strengthened regional resilience against climate change (ГЭФ. *Отчет о проектах в Центральной Азии, 2010–2020.* Вашингтон: GEF, 2021, 45 с.).

Regional Mechanisms

The Interstate Commission for Water Coordination (ICWC), established in 1992, was tasked with regulating water distribution from the Syr Darya and Amu Darya rivers. However, its effectiveness has been undermined by upstream and downstream rivalries, resulting in over 50 water-related conflicts since 2000, including violent clashes in the Fergana Valley (Вегерих, К. *Гидрогегемония в бассейне Амударьи // Водная политика.* 2008. Т. 10, Доп. 2. С. 71–88). The Asian Development Bank (ADB) has invested $300 million in irrigation modernization projects in Uzbekistan, reducing water losses by 15%. Yet, the success of such initiatives depends on interstate cooperation, which remains hampered by geopolitical fragmentation and national rivalries.

Non-Governmental Organizations (NGOs)

Non-governmental organizations have stepped in to fill governance gaps. The Regional Environmental Center for Central Asia (CAREC) has trained over 10,000 farmers in drip irrigation since 2015, reducing water use in pilot zones by 30% (РЭЦЦА. *Устойчивое водопользование в Центральной Азии: Отчет 2020.* Алматы: CAREC, 2021. 52 с.)

International NGOs such as WWF contribute to biodiversity conservation, helping increase the snow leopard population from 4,000 to 6,000 and establishing 2 million hectares of protected areas. These efforts have strengthened regional environmental diplomacy (WWF. *Сохранение биоразнообразия Центральной Азии: Отчет 2022.* Гланд: WWF, 2023. 38 с.).

Scientific Communities

Academic and scientific institutions also play a vital role. Organizations such as the Academy of Sciences of Uzbekistan and Kazakh National University conduct climate modelling, projecting a 10–15 km³ annual decline in glacial runoff. These studies are critical for justifying adaptation measures and guiding negotiations with international donors (IPCC. *Climate Change 2021: The Physical Science Basis.* Cambridge: Cambridge University Press, 2021. p. 2391). However, the impact of NGOs and research institutions is constrained by funding shortages, political restrictions and weak integration into state policies. Their reliance on external support underscores the region's institutional fragility.

Innovative Solutions and Future Scenarios

Addressing environmental insecurity in Central Asia requires a combination of technological innovation, improved governance, and stronger regional cooperation. Several solutions have been piloted, yet their long-term effectiveness depends on structural reforms and sustained political commitment.

Alternative Water Governance

Water stress is the region's most critical challenge. Annual losses of 10–15 km³ in the Syr Darya and Amu Darya rivers, caused by accelerated glacial melting and irrigation inefficiencies (up to 40%) demand a shift from outdated allocation models to Integrated Water

Resources Management (IWRM). This basin-wide approach emphasizes joint planning among riparian states, equitable distribution, and the incorporation of ecological sustainability into water policies. Pilot initiatives, such as the introduction of drip irrigation in Uzbekistan, have reduced water consumption by 30% in test zones. However, scaling IWRM requires transnational institutions with greater regulatory authority and significant political will to overcome geopolitical fragmentation.

Renewable Energy Transition

Expanding renewable energy sources (RES) offers a pathway to reduce dependence on fossil fuels and ease ecological pressures. Kazakhstan has increased RES to 10% of its energy mix by 2025, with projects such as the 100 MW Kapshagay solar power plant reducing CO_2 emissions by 1 million tons annually (*Министерство энергетики РК. Развитие возобновляемых источников энергии: Отчет 2025.* – Астана: Минэнерго, 2025. – 40 с.).

The region possesses enormous renewable potential: Uzbekistan receives up to 2,200 kWh/m² of solar radiation annually, while Kazakhstan's wind resources are estimated at 920 billion kWh per year. However, large-scale deployment requires around $1 billion in investment per country, comprehensive energy reforms, and overcoming resistance from entrenched coal lobbies. Coordinated support from global financial institutions such as the ADB is essential to sustain this transition.

Environmental Education and Public Awareness

A legacy of Soviet industrialization has left the region with low ecological awareness. Although NGOs such as CAREC have trained more than 10,000 farmers in sustainable practices, outreach remains limited. Government-led efforts are emerging, Uzbekistan introduced environmental education into school curricula in 2020, but currently reach only 15% of students due to budget shortages and a lack of qualified teachers.

Public engagement through media campaigns and awareness programs could expand societal participation. However, in authoritarian systems such as Turkmenistan, state-controlled narratives often suppress open discussion on ecological issues.

Building a culture of environmental responsibility remains essential to ensure long-term sustainability.

Future Scenarios

Optimistic Scenario: Integration and Ecological Modernization

This scenario envisions strengthened regional cooperation in water management through an empowered ICWC and the establishment of a unified intergovernmental environmental body. By 2050, renewable energy reaches 30% of the energy mix, reducing greenhouse gas emissions by 40%. Environmental education programs target at least 50% of the population by 2030, raising ecological awareness and fostering sustainable consumption. Political prerequisites include stronger regional institutions, expanded international financing, multilateral agreements modelled on the Paris Agreement, and private-sector engagement via public-private partnerships (PPPs).

Pessimistic Scenario: Institutional Stagnation and Ecosystem Collapse

In the absence of reforms, water disputes intensify as glaciers retreat and droughts worsen. Food imports increase by 30%, undermining food security. WHO models predict a 50% rise in disease incidence by 2050 due to higher pollution and water scarcity. Desertification expands to cover 50% of land, collapsing traditional agro-ecological systems and driving mass migration. Politically, this scenario is marked by institutional paralysis, fragmented policies, underfunded conservation programs, rising protest movements, and declining public trust in governments.

Realistic Scenario: Localized Success without Regional Synergy

In this middle-ground scenario, moderate progress occurs in individual states, particularly Kazakhstan and Uzbekistan, in renewable energy adoption, irrigation efficiency, and sustainable agriculture. However, interstate cooperation remains weak, with fragmented initiatives producing only localized improvements. Without effective transboundary mechanisms, long-term sustainability is uncertain.

Conclusion and Recommendations

The future of environmental security in Central Asia hinges on political choices in three interconnected domains: water governance, energy transition, and regional cooperation. While the region faces severe ecological challenges, including the desiccation of the Aral Sea, desertification, biodiversity loss, radioactive contamination, and the accelerating effects of climate change, these crises also present opportunities for transformative reform. The central obstacles remain institutional fragmentation, weak regulatory enforcement, and competing national interests that undermine cooperative frameworks. Overcoming these barriers requires both strengthened domestic capacity and a commitment to regional integration. Without unified governance, Central Asia risks sliding further into ecological decline, social instability, and economic dependency.

Key Recommendations

Establish a Supranational Water Governance Body

i) Empower the Interstate Commission for Water Coordination (ICWC) or create a new regional authority with binding decision-making powers.

ii) Prioritize Integrated Water Resources Management (IWRM) to ensure equitable water allocation between upstream hydropower producers and downstream agricultural economies.

1. *Expand Investment in Renewable Energy*
    i) Scale up renewable energy deployment, aiming for a 30% share of the energy mix by 2050.
    ii) Partner with international financial institutions (ADB, World Bank, GEF) to secure funding and technical expertise.
    iii) Reduce reliance on coal, which still accounts for 70% of Kazakhstan's energy balance, by implementing phased policy reforms.

2. *Implement Environmental Education and Public Awareness Programs*
    i) Expand environmental curricula to reach at least 50% of school-age populations by 2030.

ii) Promote grassroots engagement through NGOs and media campaigns to build ecological responsibility at the societal level.
iii) Support community-based initiatives such as drip irrigation training and biodiversity conservation programs.

3. *Enhance Monitoring and Data Systems*
   i) Invest in satellite-based tracking and automated monitoring stations to improve transparency and early-warning capacity.
   ii) Share environmental data across borders to build trust and enable coordinated responses to crises such as floods, droughts, and toxic storms.

4. *Strengthen International Partnerships*
   i) Engage actively with UNDP, WHO, UNEP, and regional NGOs to bridge financial and institutional gaps.
   ii) Leverage public-private partnerships (PPPs) to mobilize green investment and accelerate the adoption of innovative technologies.

An Assessment

Central Asia stands at a critical crossroads. Without decisive reform, ecological degradation will continue to fuel public health crises, food insecurity, migration pressures, and regional instability. However, with coordinated political will, investment in sustainable technologies, and stronger international partnerships, the region can transform environmental vulnerability into an opportunity for resilience and sustainable development.

REFERENCES

FAO. The State of the World's Land and Water Resources for Food and Agriculture. – Rome: FAO, 2021. 394 p.

Glantz M. H. Creeping Environmental Problems and Sustainable Development in the Aral Sea Basin. Cambridge: Cambridge University Press, 1999. – 304 p.

IAEA. Radiological Conditions in the Areas Affected by Uranium Mining and Milling in Central Asia. Vienna: International Atomic Energy Agency, 2015. 89 p.

IPCC. Climate Change 2021: The Physical Science Basis / Ed. by V. Masson-Delmotte et al. Cambridge: Cambridge University Press, 2021. 2391 p.

IPCC. Климатические изменения 2021: Физическая основа / Под ред. В. Массон-Дельмотт и др. Кембридж: Cambridge University Press, 2021. 2391 с.

IUCN. The IUCN Red List of Threatened Species. – Gland: IUCN, 2022. URL: https://www.iucnredlist.org (дата обращения: 25.03.2025).

UNECE. Second Assessment of Transboundary Rivers, Lakes and Groundwaters. – Geneva: United Nations, 2011. 448 p.

WHO. Ambient Air Pollution: A Global Assessment of Exposure and Burden of Disease. – Geneva: World Health Organization, 2016. – 121 p.

WWF. Сохранение биоразнообразия Центральной Азии: Отчет 2022. Гланд: WWF, 2023. 38 с.

Вегерих, К. Гидрогегемония в бассейне Амударьи // Водная политика. 2008. – Т. 10, Доп. 2. С. 71–88.

ВОЗ. Загрязнение атмосферного воздуха: Глобальная оценка воздействия и бремени болезней. Женева: Всемирная организация здравоохранения, 2016. 121 с.

ВОЗ. Загрязнение атмосферного воздуха: Глобальная оценка воздействия и бремени болезней. Женева: ВОЗ, 2016. – 121 с.

ГЭФ. Отчет о проектах в Центральной Азии, 2010–2020. Вашингтон: GEF, 2021. 45 с.

Деградация земель в Центральной Азии [Электронный ресурс] // CAWater-Info. URL: https://www.cawater-info.net/bk/water_land_resourcesuse/russian ver/pdf/15.pdf (дата обращения: 25.03.2025).

ЕЭК ООН. Вторая оценка трансграничных рек, озер и подземных вод. Женева: Организация Объединенных Наций, 2011. 448 с.

ЕЭК ООН. Вторая оценка трансграничных рек, озер и подземных вод. Женева: ООН, 2011. 448 с.

Изменение климата на Тянь-Шане в голоцене и проблема... // Известия РАН. Серия географическая. URL: https://izvestia.igras.ru/jour/article/download/ 342/335.

МАГАТЭ. Радиологические условия в районах, затронутых добычей и переработкой урана в Центральной Азии. – Вена: Международное агентство по атомной энергии, 2015. 89 с.

Миклин, П. Катастрофа Аральского моря // Ежегодный обзор наук о Земле и планетах. 2007. Т. 35. С. 47–72.

Миклин, П. Катастрофа Аральского моря // Ежегодный обзор наук о Земле и планетах. – 2007. – Т. 35. – С. 47–72.

Министерство энергетики РК. Развитие возобновляемых источников энергии: Отчет 2025. Астана: Минэнерго, 2025. – 40 с.

МСОП. Красный список видов, находящихся под угрозой [Электронный ресурс] // IUCN. URL: https://www.iucnredlist.org (дата обращения: 25.03.2025).

Национальная стратегия развития Республики Таджикистан до 2030 года. Душанбе: Правительство РТ, 2016. – 96 с.

Национальная стратегия устойчивого развития Туркменистана до 2040 года. Ашхабад: Правительство ТМ, 2020. 36 с.

Природные экосистемы стран Центральной Азии стремительно разрушаются [Электронный ресурс] // CABAR.asia. – URL: https://cabar.asia/ru/ prirodn ye-ekosis temy-stran-tsentralnoj-azii-stremitelno-razrushayutsya (дата обращения: 25.03.2025).

Программа реабилитации территорий, пострадавших от урановых отходов. Бишкек: Правительство КР, 2018. – 28 с.

ПРООН. Годовой отчет 2020: Центральная Азия. – Нью-Йорк: UNDP, 2021. 68 с.

РЭЦЦА. Устойчивое водопользование в Центральной Азии: Отчет 2020. Алматы: CAREC, 2021. 52 с.

Стратегия «Казахстан-2050»: Новый политический курс состоявшегося государства. – Астана: Правительство РК, 2013. 48 с.

Стратегия действий по пяти приоритетным направлениям развития Республики Узбекистан в 2017–2021 годах. Ташкент: Кабинет Министров РУ, 2017. 32 с.

ФАО. Состояние земельных и водных ресурсов мира для продовольствия и сельского хозяйства. – Рим: ФАО, 2021. 394 с.

Центральная Азия // Большая российская энциклопедия. URL: https://bigenc.ru/c/tsentral-naia-aziia-ef669e.

Центральная Азия: География, Климат и Культура // Бегемот. URL: https://begemot.ai/projects/2007169-centralnaia-aziia-geografiia-klimat-i-kultura.

10

Uzbekistan in the Process of Central Asian Integration

Omonboy Khaytimmatov

ABSTRACT

Regional integration in Central Asia has gained renewed significance in recent years. As the most populous country and a key transit hub in the region, Uzbekistan plays a crucial role in shaping integration processes. This chapter examines Uzbekistan's engagement in Central Asia's regional integration through political, economic, and infrastructural initiatives. It highlights key efforts under President Shavkat Mirziyoyev's leadership, focusing on strengthened diplomatic relations, financial liberalization, and major connectivity projects. The study also discusses challenges to deeper integration, including geopolitical complexities, economic disparities, and infrastructural limitations. By analysing Uzbekistan's engagement in regional organizations such as the Shanghai Cooperation Organization (SCO) and its relations with neighbouring states, the chapter provides a comprehensive outlook on Uzbekistan's role in regional cooperation. The final section offers policy recommendations for enhancing regional stability and economic growth.

Keywords: *Uzbekistan, Central Asia, regional integration, economic cooperation, diplomacy, connectivity, SCO.*

Regional integration stands as a cornerstone for unlocking the potential of Central Asia, a region historically renowned as a crossroads of civilizations along the Silk Road. Today, the five nations of Kazakhstan, Kyrgyzstan, Tajikistan, Turkmenistan, and Uzbekistan face a shared imperative to harness integration for economic development, security, and stability. The importance of this endeavour cannot be overstated: cohesive regional efforts promise to bolster trade, enhance infrastructure, and secure collective prosperity in a part of the world where isolation has too often hindered progress. Central Asia confronts common challenges that underscore the need for unity, resource management complexities, such as water distribution, persistent trade barriers that limit market access, and infrastructure deficits that impede connectivity. However, within this landscape of opportunity and necessity, Uzbekistan emerges as a pivotal force, leveraging its unique attributes to drive the region toward a more integrated future.

Uzbekistan's strategic position in Central Asia is unrivalled. As the only country in the region sharing borders with all four of its neighbours, it serves as a natural transit hub, facilitating the flow of goods, energy, and ideas across a landlocked expanse. With a population exceeding 35 million, the largest in Central Asia, Uzbekistan commands significant human capital, underpinning its role as a regional leader. Its economy, diversified across agriculture, energy, and manufacturing, provides a robust foundation for fostering economic ties. Uzbekistan's economic diversification includes a 10% increase in gas exports via the Central Asia and China pipeline in 2023, reflecting its global outreach (International Energy Agency, 2023).

Since 2016, under the visionary leadership of President Shavkat Mirziyoyev, Uzbekistan has embraced a transformative agenda, shifting from the inward-looking policies of the past to a proactive stance of regional engagement. This shift has revitalized Uzbekistan's historical legacy as a connector, positioning it at the forefront of efforts to weave Central Asia into a cohesive economic and security framework.

The importance of regional integration in Central Asia lies in its capacity to address shared challenges and unlock collective potential. Economically, integration promises to dismantle trade barriers, enabling Uzbekistan's cotton, gas, and textile exports to reach broader markets while fostering mutual growth with neighbours. In terms of security, a united approach strengthens defences against transnational threats like terrorism and trafficking, particularly given the region's proximity to Afghanistan. Stability, too hinges on cooperation, whether through synchronized infrastructure projects or joint resource management, to ensure equitable development across borders. Uzbekistan's central location amplifies its influence in these domains, making it a linchpin for initiatives that span the region, from transport corridors to energy grids.

This chapter tried to focus on Uzbekistan's approach to regional integration, exploring how its policies and actions shape the trajectory of Central Asian cooperation. The purpose is to illuminate Uzbekistan's contributions across political, economic, and security spheres, assessing both the opportunities it seizes and the challenges it navigates. Politically, Uzbekistan's diplomatic outreach has rebuilt trust with neighbours, fostering dialogue where tensions once prevailed. Economically, its infrastructure investments and trade initiatives signal a commitment to connectivity, while in security, its leadership within frameworks like the Shanghai Cooperation Organisation (SCO) reinforces regional resilience. The scope encompasses Uzbekistan's post-2016 evolution, drawing on qualitative data from policy documents, economic reports, and scholarly analyses. By highlighting Uzbekistan's strategic role, this chapter underscores its capacity to lead Central Asia toward a future of shared prosperity and stability, building on its geographic and demographic strengths to overcome regional hurdles.

REFERENCES

Acharya, A. (2014). Constructing a security community in Southeast Asia. Routledge.

Asian Development Bank. (2024). Central Asia Outlook 2024. ADB Publications.

Central Asia Barometer. (2022). Regional integration survey 2022. CAB Reports.

Cooley, A. (2017). Uzbekistan's new foreign policy. Foreign Affairs.

Eurasian Economic Commission. (2023). EAEU annual report 2023. EEC Publications.

Freedom House. (2023). Nations in transit 2023. https://freedomhouse.org

Haas, E. B. (1964). Beyond the nation-state: Functionalism and international organization. Stanford University Press.

International Energy Agency. (2023). Energy Outlook 2023. IEA Publications.

International Monetary Fund. (2023). Central Asia Economic Review 2023. IMF Publications.

Laruelle, M. (2021). Russia and China in Central Asia. Central Asian Survey, 40(3), 321–339.

Mattli, W. (1999). The logic of regional integration. Cambridge University Press.

Moravcsik, A. (1993). Preferences and power in the European Community. Journal of Common Market Studies, 31(4), 473–524.

Radio Free Europe. (2022, July 15). Uzbekistan, Tajikistan sign power project deal. https://www.rferl.org

SCO Secretariat. (2022). Samarkand Declaration. SCO Official Documents.

U.S. Department of State. (2023). Central Asia strategy 2023. https://www.state.gov

Uzbekistan Ministry of Economy. (2023). Annual economic report 2023. Tashkent.

Uzbekistan Ministry of Foreign Affairs. (2022). Foreign policy doctrine 2022. Tashkent.

Uzbekistan Ministry of Labor. (2023). Labor migration report 2023. Tashkent.

World Bank. (2024). Central Asia economic update. World Bank Group.

Xinhua. (2022, July 27). Uzbekistan hosts SCO talks on Afghanistan. http://www.xinhua net.com

Xinhua. (2023, August 10). CKU corridor advances in Tashkent. http://www.xinhuanet.com

11

Fundamental and Applied Problems of the Integration of Central Asian Countries

Zakir Usmanov

ABSTRACT

This chapter examines the challenges and prospects of integration processes in Central Asia, which exert a significant influence on the region's developmental trajectory. The necessity of regional integration arises from intensifying geopolitical and geo-economic turbulence worldwide, dynamics that no single state in the region can address independently. Equally pressing is the need to ensure security, preserve territorial integrity, and overcome geopolitical isolation by jointly developing transport and logistics infrastructure.

Although regional integration trends have gained momentum in recent years, attempts to institutionalize multilateral cooperation have yet to produce a comprehensive and fully functioning integration association. Central Asian countries remain in search of an effective model of regional interaction. Consequently, identifying both fundamental and applied problems and adopting a differentiated approach to their resolution is crucial for defining integration strategies, mechanisms, and tools, thereby enhancing the effectiveness of integration processes.

Keywords: *Central Asia, regional integration, geopolitics, fundamental problems, applied problems, geographical factor, economic factor, historical factor.*

Introduction

Central Asia, a vast geographical region located at the heart of Eurasia, spans approximately 4 million square kilometres and is home to around 80 million people. Its geopolitical importance is derived from its position between the Heartland and the Rimland, zones of enduring global geopolitical rivalry. The region's strategic significance lies not only in its role as a bridge between Europe and Asia but also in its vast reserves of energy resources, rare earth metals, and vital trade routes.

Since independence, the Central Asian states have undergone profound transformations across economic, social, political, military, cultural, and ideological domains. These multifaceted processes, broadly described as "nation-state building", have unfolded at varying paces across the region, while simultaneously interacting with ongoing regional integration efforts. Thus, the processes of national self-identification coexist with attempts at regional unification.

Historical Perspectives on Integration

Political scientist F. Tolipov (2005) emphasizes that throughout history, integration and disintegration in Central Asia have often overlapped, creating a complex geo-socio-cultural-political structure in which national and regional identities are difficult to disentangle. He observes that processes of national self-identification have consistently manifested in various supranational, integrative quasi-polities, from the empires of Genghis Khan and Timur, to the Bukhara Emirate, the Kokand and Khiva Khanates, Turan, Turkestan, Tsarist Russia, the USSR (through the concept of "Middle Asia and Kazakhstan"), and post-Soviet structures such as the CAEC/CACO and the CIS itself (Tolipov, 2005).

Similarly, as Alieva notes, the collapse of the USSR provided Kazakhstan, Kyrgyzstan, Tajikistan, Turkmenistan, and Uzbekistan the opportunity to chart independent developmental paths and become subjects of international relations. Yet, in the early years, these states encountered enormous difficulties in integrating into global political and economic systems. Their challenges stemmed largely from transitional conditions, including unstable political institutions and underdeveloped national economies still in their formative stages.

Contemporary Geopolitical Context

The intensification of global geopolitical turbulence and the emergence of a new world order continue to directly and indirectly affect the socio-economic development and security of Central Asian states. This situation necessitates identifying the conditions for integration, defining key obstacles, and formulating effective policies for advancing integration. Despite efforts, unresolved legacies of the Soviet period, such as disputed borders and conflicts over water and energy resources, have hindered integration. These issues, coupled with lingering misconceptions about the region, led many experts to predict negative outcomes for Central Asia's post-independence development. Analysts, including Zbigniew Brzezinski (1997), warned of potential disintegration, internal conflicts, economic collapse, and "Balkanization."

Tolipov (2001) also highlights critical obstacles to regional integration, such as information warfare, destructive geopolitical strategies, inflated perceptions of national interest, weak democratic institutions, autocratic governance, mistrust, fears of "Uzbek hegemony," and perceived rivalry between Uzbekistan and Kazakhstan. Nonetheless, recent political changes, particularly the leadership transition in Uzbekistan in 2016, catalysed renewed cooperation. As Dmitry Li (2017) observes, this period fostered greater collaboration among Central Asian states to address regional issues, with Uzbekistan emphasizing shared civilizational heritage, economic and security interdependence, collective approaches to water and energy challenges, and the resolution of border disputes. In this context, Tajikistan's Foreign Minister Hamrokhon Zarifi (2010) stresses that integration is not only a contemporary global trend but also a necessity for Central Asia, describing it as a fundamental principle of international relations and a powerful driver of development.

Fundamental Problems of Integration

Geographical Factor

Geographic isolation constitutes a primary challenge to integration. Central Asia remains largely disconnected from major global economic centers and transport corridors. For instance, freight transportation between the EU and China predominantly traverses Russia or maritime routes, bypassing Central Asia. Consequently, most states in the region, except Kazakhstan, are excluded from lucrative transit flows, which limits foreign investment and constrains socio-economic development. This isolation dates back to the 16th century, when maritime trade routes diminished the region's connectivity. Russian imperial expansion and later Soviet centralization deepened its role as a peripheral resource base within a closed economic system.

Historical Factor

Beginning in the 16th century, Central Asian polities experienced political, economic, and technological decline, transforming from active geopolitical actors into passive objects of external domination. Tsarist conquest and Soviet control institutionalized this dependency.

Ermek Baisalov argues that the administrative territorial reforms imposed by Moscow in the 1920s, following a "divide and rule" principle, cemented present-day borders. These artificial boundaries split ethnic groups across republics, creating disputes that still undermine cooperation (Cabar Asia, 2021). Notably, the recent historic border agreement between Kyrgyzstan and Tajikistan (Tengrinews, 2024) represents progress toward resolving such disputes and advancing integration.

Economic Factor

Economic asymmetries further complicate integration. Historically, Central Asian economies were structured to serve Soviet metropolitan interests, leaving enduring imbalances. While Kazakhstan and Uzbekistan have recorded notable GDP growth since independence, the region's collective share of the global economy remains below one percent. Economic complexity also remains low. However, Uzbekistan is demonstrating a steady rise in industrial diversification. Although cooperation in mechanical engineering, textiles, and other sectors are growing, current industrial capacities are insufficient to underpin full-scale integration.

Applied Problems of Integration

Beyond structural obstacles, applied problems limit integration in cultural, educational, scientific, and social spheres. Despite shared historical and cultural ties, the region lacks unified cultural, scientific, educational, tourism, and sports spaces. The EU experience illustrates the significance of such integration. Initiatives like the "e-Europe" program (2000) and the Schengen Area exemplify how shared informational, educational, and mobility frameworks can strengthen unity. Central Asia would benefit from similar measures, such as regional cultural funds, joint educational institutions, cross-border media platforms, and integrated tourism initiatives.

Conclusion and Findings

Integration among Central Asian states is essential for achieving sustainable socio-economic development and ensuring security amid geopolitical turbulence. To this end, a differentiated approach is necessary, distinguishing between fundamental and applied challenges. Fundamental problems, geographical isolation, historical legacies, and economic imbalances, require long-term strategies, substantial financial resources, and time horizons of at least 10–20 years. Addressing these involves developing roadmaps for economic complexity, industrial cooperation, and financial mechanisms similar to the Uzbek-Kyrgyz Development Fund. Applied problems, by contrast, can be addressed more quickly through initiatives in education, culture, science, tourism, and sports, supported by regional institutions such as universities and media platforms.

REFERENCES

Aliyeva, R. R. (n.d.). Integration as a factor of sustainable development and stability of Central Asian states. Political Problems of International Relations, Global and Regional Development.

Brzezinski, Z. (1997). The grand chessboard: American primacy and its geostrategic imperatives.

Cabar. Asia. (2021). Territorial disputes in Central Asia on the eve of the 30th anniversary of independence. Retrieved from https://cabar.asia/ru/territorialnye-spory-v-tsentralnoj-azii-na-poroge-30-letiya-nezavisimosti

Dieter, H. (1996). Regional integration in Central Asia: Current economic position and prospects. Central Asian Survey, 15(3-4), 369-386.

Golovnin, M., Zaharov, A., & Ushkalova, D. (2016). Economic integration: Lessons for the post-Soviet area. Mirovaia ekonomika i mezhdunarodnye otnosheniia, 60(4), 61-69. (In Russian)

Li, D. (2017, May 30). Central Asian integration: More real than ever? Retrieved from https://astanatimes.com/2017/05/central-asian-integration-more-real-than-ever/

Molle, W. (1994). The economics of European integration: Theory, practice, policy. Dartmouth.

Pavlyutenkova, M. Y. (2006). Electronic government: Western experience in the Russian projection. Internet and Modern Society: Eleventh All-Russian Unified Conference. Retrieved from http://www.infosoc.ru/2006/thes/Pavlyutenkova.pdf

Sadru, H. A. (1997). Integration in Central Asia: From theory to policy. Central Asian Survey, 16(4), 573-586.

Tengrinews. (2024). Kyrgyzstan and Tajikistan signed a historic agreement. Retrieved from https://tengrinews.kz/sng/kyirgyizstan-tadjikistan-podpisali-istoricheskoe-soglashenie-563294/

Tovias, A. (1994). A survey of the theory of economic integration. In H. Michelmann & P. Soldatos (Eds.), European integration: Theories and approaches (p. 57). University Press of America.

Tolipov, F. (2001). Nationalism as a geopolitical phenomenon: The Central Asian case. Central Asian Survey, 20(2).

Tolipov, F. (2005). Central Asia as a space, polity, people, and destiny. Central Asia and the Caucasus, 2(38), 121.

Umarova, N. (n.d.). What does the extension of transport corridors in Afghanistan mean for Central Asia? Retrieved from https://www.cacianalyst.org/resources/0307Nargiza_ feature.pdf

UNESCAP. (n.d.). TransContainer [PDF file]. Retrieved from https://www.unescap.org/ sites/default/files/TransContainer.pdf

Zakhirova, L. (2013). The international politics of water security in Central Asia. Europe-Asia Studies, 65(10), 1994-2013.

Zarifi, H. (2010). Multivector diplomacy of Tajikistan. Offset.

12

The Principle of Justice in the Reforms of Central Asian Countries: A Guarantee of Peace and Security

Hamroyev Saidjon Sanoyevich

ABSTRACT

South and Central Asia represent regions of profound geopolitical, economic, and cultural significance. In recent years, these areas have faced global and regional security challenges, questions of social justice, and notable geopolitical transformations. At Uzbekistan's initiative, annual consultative meetings among Central Asian states have been established to strengthen cooperation, fostering a new political environment for ensuring both regional security and economic collaboration. Critical issues such as equitable resource distribution, environmental management, and water governance have acquired growing importance. Meanwhile, the involvement of global powers, particularly the United States, China, and Russia, has intensified competition, thereby aggravating security concerns.

Against this backdrop, regional stability depends on deepened cooperation, the promotion of social justice, and sustainable economic development. Achieving social justice requires equipping younger generations with modern knowledge, reducing economic inequality, and fostering civic engagement. Pragmatic policies and mutually beneficial collaboration among states further contribute to maintaining regional peace and prosperity. This chapter examines geopolitical shifts, regional security challenges, and social justice in Central Asia. It explores threats such as competition among global powers, terrorism, territorial disputes, and economic inequality. It also highlights the role of education, economic development, and civil society in advancing social justice. The chapter underscores the importance of collective efforts to maintain regional stability and resolve pressing social issues.

Keywords: *Geopolitical shifts, regional security, social justice, terrorism, territorial conflicts, economic inequality, regional cooperation, stability*

Introduction

Historically, Central Asia has been recognized as a region of strategic geopolitical, economic, and cultural importance. In recent decades, however, shifting geopolitical dynamics, mounting global and regional security concerns, and unresolved issues of social justice have posed new challenges for the states of the region. While these transformations open opportunities for enhanced cooperation and development, they also present considerable risks. On Uzbekistan's initiative, annual consultative meetings of Central Asian leaders have become institutionalized. These gatherings serve as a constructive platform for regional dialogue, enabling states to discuss shared problems and adopt collective solutions. Prominent areas of collaboration include joint industrial projects, energy cooperation, infrastructure development, food security, climate change adaptation, and the promotion of cultural and humanitarian ties.

Nevertheless, growing competition among major global powers, including the United States, China, and Russia, poses risks to the region's stability. This rivalry directly influences the political and economic security of Central Asian states. Safeguarding peace in such a climate requires strengthening both domestic resilience and regional and international cooperation.

Literature Review

The question of Central Asian integration has been widely studied by regional leaders and scholars. Among the most influential voices are President Shavkat Mirziyoyev, First President Islam Karimov, and specialists such as F. Ravshanov, Q. Nazarov, S. Otamurodov, B. Omonov, G. Ochilovaz, and S. G'ofurov.

Research Methodology

This study conducted through logical and comparative methods, including historicism, synthesis, generalization, and analysis, to examine the essence of justice within Central Asian reforms.

Central Asia in the 21st Century Global Order

The 21st century global order is defined by multipolarity, multiculturalism, pluralism, religious tolerance, globalization, and integration. No state today remains unaffected by these processes; even countries reluctant to participate in international organizations experience their consequences. Ironically, attempts to remain isolated often expose such nations to greater risks.The collapse of the Soviet Union transformed Central Asia into a competitive geopolitical arena. Comprising Kazakhstan, Kyrgyzstan, Tajikistan, Turkmenistan, and Uzbekistan, the region emerged as a collective actor in international relations. Yet, its socio-economic challenges, ranging from poverty and healthcare deficits to unemployment and migration, continue to undermine political stability. Uzbekistan has prioritized the creation of a peaceful and stable regional environment. President Shavkat Mirziyoyev has repeatedly emphasized strengthening relations with neighboring states, advancing cooperation, and jointly addressing security concerns.

Regional Cooperation and Consultative Meetings

Since 2016, Uzbekistan has played a central role in shaping regional dialogue. The consultative meetings of Central Asian leaders, initiated in Astana in 2018, marked a turning point. Agreements were reached on expanding security mechanisms, developing roadmaps for trade and innovation, and forming joint positions on pressing international issues. Subsequently, UN resolutions adopted in 2019 highlighted the importance of regional cooperation in sustainable development, climate action, and tourism. These measures enhanced the global presence of Central Asian states while encouraging mutual trust. Trade statistics further reflect this growing cooperation. By 2024, Uzbekistan's foreign trade turnover with Central Asia reached $7 billion, with significant growth in joint ventures and regional trade volumes. Such outcomes demonstrate the effectiveness of regional mechanisms and the tangible benefits of integration.

Geopolitical Rivalries and Risks

The interests of major global powers heavily influence Central Asia. The United States prioritizes limiting Chinese and Russian influence, promoting democratic values, and maintaining security through military partnerships. China, through its Belt and Road initiative, seeks to enhance regional infrastructure and economic cooperation, though this raises concerns about sovereignty. Russia, meanwhile relies on historical ties, military cooperation, and energy integration to maintain its regional influence. The competition among these powers poses challenges for Central Asian stability, often exacerbating socio-economic inequalities and fuelling security risks. For regional states, the path forward lies in deepening pragmatic cooperation and safeguarding justice as a principle of integration.

The Principle of Justice in Regional Reforms

Justice understood as fairness, integrity, and respect for rights, plays a central role in regional reforms. Its application ensures political equality, economic fairness, and social stability. Political Justice strengthens trust and dialogue among states, reinforcing peace. Economic Justice guarantees equitable resource distribution, supports trade, and enhances development, particularly in energy and infrastructure. Social Justice reduces inequality, expands access to education and healthcare, and promotes civil society participation. Collectively, these dimensions of justice form the basis for sustainable integration and regional stability.

Security Challenges and Joint Responses

Central Asia faces multifaceted security threats, including terrorism, extremism, territorial disputes, and socio-economic disparities. Addressing these requires both political reforms and joint regional actions. Integration guided by justice provides an effective framework for combating terrorism, managing resources equitably, and fostering security cooperation. Beyond military measures, justice strengthens social and economic ties that underpin security. By investing in education, fostering entrepreneurship, and promoting youth development, states can reduce inequality and prevent instability.

Justice, Education, and Youth Development

Ensuring social justice necessitates prioritizing human capital development. Providing quality education, creating employment, and promoting civic values such as tolerance, dignity, and patriotism are essential. Equally, nurturing national pride and cultural traditions in younger generations helps reinforce stability and cohesion.

Conclusion

The integration reforms of Central Asian states, guided by the principle of justice constitute a vital foundation for peace and security in the region. Justice ensures equality in political, economic, and social spheres, while fostering cooperation that addresses terrorism, extremism, and inequality. Mutual trust, equitable economic integration, and respect for rights enable sustainable stability. Education and youth development remain central to this vision, ensuring the prosperity of future generations. Ultimately, the principle of justice is not only a moral idea but also a strategic necessity for Central Asia. It guarantees peace, strengthens inter-governmental relations, and enhances the region's role on the global stage.

REFERENCES

Jumaniyozov, X.S., Nigmanova, U.B. "Globallashuv asoslari", Textbook. Tashkent, 2020.

Jumaniyozov, X.S., Rasulova, A.M. "Ekstremizm va terrorizmga qarshi kurashning ma'naviy-ma'rifiy asoslari" Textbook. Tashkent, 2019.

Karimov, I.A. Xavfsizlik va barqaror taraqqiyot yo'lida Collected Works, Volume 6. – Tashkent: "O'zbekiston", 1998.

Mirziyoyev, Sh. "Milliy tiklanishdan – milliy yuksalish sari", Volume 4. – Tashkent: "O'zbekiston", 2020. 456 pages.

Mirziyoyev, Sh. "Xalqimizning roziligi bizning faoliyatimizga berilgan eng oliy bahodir" Volume 2. Tashkent: "O'zbekiston", 2018. – 508 pages.

Mirziyoyev, Sh.M. Milliy taraqqiyot yo'limizni qat'iyat bilan davom ettirib, yangi bosqichga ko'taramiz, Tashkent: "O'zbekiston" NMIU, 2017.

Mirziyoyev, Sh.M. Xalqimizning roziligi bizning faoliyatimizga berilgan eng oliy bahodir– Tashkent: "O'zbekiston" NMIU, 2018.

Mirziyoyev, Shavkat Miromonovich. "Hozirgi zamon va Yangi O'zbekiston Tashkent" "O'zbekiston" Publishing House, 2024. Chapter 5.

Otamurodov, S. Globallashuv va millat, Tashkent: "Yangi asr avlodi" 2008.

O'zbekiston Respublikasining Konstitutsiyasi. Tashkent: O'zbekiston Publishing House, 2023. Page 80.

Qahhorova, Sh. Global ma'naviyat – globallashuvning g'oyaviy asosi– Tashkent: "Tafakkur", 2009.

Shavkat Mirziyoyev. "Yangi O'zbekiston taraqqiyot strategiyasi", Tashkent: "O'zbekiston", 2022. 440 pages.

SECTION III

Regional Cooperation Mechanism

13

The Role of the Sanghai Cooperation Organisation in Shaping Regional Security Dynamics in Central Asia

Movkebaeva G.I. Uzakbaev

ABSTRACT

The Shanghai Cooperation Organization (SCO) plays a pivotal role in maintaining regional security in Central Asia by addressing challenges such as terrorism, border security, transnational threats, and cybersecurity. The organization fosters multilateral cooperation among its member states, including China, Russia, and the Central Asian republics, while contending with significant limitations in decision-making, geopolitical rivalries, and criticisms concerning human rights and governance. Comparisons with other regional security institutions, such as the CSTO and the OSCE, underscore both the strengths and weaknesses of the SCO's model. Looking ahead, deeper security cooperation, institutional reforms, and strategic expansion will be essential for enhancing the organization's effectiveness. This chapter explores the SCO's role, limitations, and prospects within the evolving geopolitical landscape.

Keywords: *Shanghai Cooperation Organization (SCO), regional security, counterterrorism, geopolitical strategy, China, Russia, Central Asia.*

Introduction

Central Asia occupies a region of immense geopolitical importance, serving as a strategic bridge between Europe and Asia while hosting abundant energy resources and vital trade corridors. However, the region remains vulnerable to persistent security challenges, including terrorism, separatism, border disputes, and transnational crime.

Following the dissolution of the Soviet Union, the Central Asian republics grappled with political instability, fragile economies, and weak institutional frameworks for regional governance (Rakhimov, 2010). The proximity of Afghanistan, long a hub of conflict further compounds these threats, necessitating coordinated responses from both regional and international actors.

Beyond traditional security risks, economic and environmental challenges also undermine stability. Contessi (2016) emphasizes that regional economic interdependence can mitigate conflict by fostering stability through stronger trade and infrastructure integration with neighboring Asian powers. Nonetheless, unresolved border conflicts, ethnic divisions, and the competing strategic interests of global actors continue to complicate Central Asia's security landscape, reinforcing the necessity of practical multilateral cooperation.

In this context, regional frameworks such as the Eurasian Economic Union (EAEU), the Collective Security Treaty Organization (CSTO), and the SCO have played an instrumental role in shaping security and economic policies. Among these, the SCO stands out for its comprehensive approach, integrating security cooperation, economic development, and political dialogue (Alimov, 2018). Its institutional mechanisms, such as the Regional Anti-Terrorist Structure (RATS), have enabled intelligence sharing and joint counterterrorism initiatives, while its broader agenda recognizes the intrinsic link between security and economic stability (Golobokov, 2015; Jackson & Shepotylo, 2024).

Theoretical Framework and Methodology

Regional security is shaped by political, economic, and military factors, with collective security serving as the organizing principle of multilateral institutions. The SCO exemplifies this principle, particularly through RATS, which enables intelligence sharing and joint counterterrorism efforts. International organizations play a crucial role in mitigating threats by institutionalizing dialogue and conflict-resolution mechanisms. The SCO's initiatives in counterterrorism, border management, and economic collaboration highlight its role as a stabilizing force in Central Asia. Jackson and Shepotylo (2024) further argue that economic interdependence reinforces stability, aligning with the SCO's emphasis on development led security.

Theoretical perspectives help explain the SCO's trajectory. Realism underscores its role as an instrument for regional powers like China and Russia to advance their strategic interests (Contessi, 2016). Regionalism highlights its function as a cooperative bloc addressing shared challenges. Methodologically, this chapter used are mainly document Analysis, reviewing SCO charters, reports, and agreements. Literature review, examining academic debates on security and multilateralism Comparative analysis, assessing if the SCO is relative to NATO, CSTO, and OSCE. Case Studies, evaluating SCO led counterterrorism, border security, and economic initiatives.

SCO's Role in Addressing Security Challenges in Central Asia

The SCO addresses a broad spectrum of security threats in the region:

1. *Counterterrorism:* Through RATS, headquartered in Tashkent, the SCO facilitates intelligence-sharing, joint training, and operational coordination. Regular multinational counterterrorism drills enhance interoperability (Rakhimov, 2010).
2. *Border Security:* The SCO promotes coordinated patrols, intelligence-sharing, and anti-trafficking measures to combat illicit flows of narcotics, arms, and human trafficking (Golobokov, 2015; Hao et al., 2023).
3. *Conflict Prevention:* By offering a diplomatic platform for dispute resolution, the SCO fosters dialogue and confidence-building among member states. Its principles of sovereignty and non-interference create a conducive environment for peaceful settlement (Contessi, 2016).
4. *Cybersecurity and Hybrid Threats:* Recognizing emerging risks, the SCO has advanced joint agreements on cybersecurity, intelligence collaboration, and countering online extremism (Hao et al., 2023). Strategic communication frameworks also address disinformation and external interference.

Limitations and Criticism

Despite its achievements, the SCO faces notable constraints:

1. *Consensus Decision-Making:* While inclusive, this slows response to crises and reflects divergent national interests (Alimov, 2018).
2. *Internal Rivalries:* Border disputes and resource competition among Central Asian states persist, while Sino-Russian competition creates strategic tensions (Andronova & Savkovich, 2015).
3. *India–Pakistan Rivalry:* Their inclusion since 2017 has added legitimacy but also complicated decision-making, as bilateral disputes occasionally undermine collective goals (Sandole, 2007).
4. *Weak Enforcement:* Unlike NATO or CSTO, the SCO lacks binding defense guarantees or centralized command structures, limiting its ability to respond militarily (Somzhurek et al., 2018).
5. *Human Rights Concerns:* The SCO has been criticized for prioritizing state sovereignty and regime stability over democratic governance and human rights (Jackson & Shepotylo, 2024). Its counterterrorism policies have been accused of legitimizing authoritarian crackdowns, particularly in China's Xinjiang and in Russia's Central Asian sphere (Andronova & Savkovich, 2015).

Political and Strategic Interests of Member States

1. *China:* Focuses on countering separatism in Xinjiang, advancing the Belt and Road Initiative (BRI), and ensuring secure borders. It leverages the SCO to extend economic and infrastructural influence while countering Western presence.
2. *Russia:* Seeks to preserve its historical sphere of influence, provide security through military bases and training, and balances China's economic dominance with initiatives like the EAEU.
3. *Central Asian States:* Engages in the SCO to enhance security, attract investment, and balance relations between Russia and China. Among Central Asian States, Kazakhstan leads in economic integration, while Uzbekistan has sought diversification through reforms. India and Pakistan: Their membership reflects the SCO's expanded Eurasian scope.

India uses it to balance China, while Pakistan strengthens its partnership with Beijing, particularly via CPEC.

4. *Observers (Iran, Afghanistan, Belarus):* Their involvement extends SCO's strategic footprint. Iran's accession enhances energy security, while Afghanistan's status underscores SCO's role in managing post-conflict stability.

Future Prospects and Strategic Developments

The SCO's effectiveness will depend on strengthening institutional mechanisms, including:

1. Expanding the scope and capacity of RATS.
2. Considering a permanent peacekeeping force.
3. Deepening border and cybersecurity cooperation.
4. Balancing expansion with decision-making efficiency.
5. Enhancing multilateral partnerships with CSTO and EAEU.

Iran's recent accession and potential candidates such as Turkey illustrate the SCO's growing geopolitical reach. However, expansion also risks diluting cohesion if new members diverge on security and economic priorities.

Conclusion

The Shanghai Cooperation Organization has established itself as a significant regional actor in Central Asia's security architecture. Through counterterrorism cooperation, border management, and responses to hybrid threats, it has enhanced stability. Yet, persistent challenges, ranging from internal rivalries and slow decision-making to criticisms over human rights, limit its effectiveness. The SCO's future lies in its ability to deepen institutional capacity, balance major power interests, and adapt to emerging threats. Its multidimensional approach, encompassing security, economics, and diplomacy, positions it as a central actor in Eurasian stability. However, its long-term legitimacy will depend on reconciling state-centric priorities with broader commitments to governance, rights, and inclusive cooperation.

REFERENCES

Alimov, R. (2018). The Shanghai Cooperation Organization: Its role and place in the global security architecture. *Journal of Eurasian Studies*, 9(2), 114–124. https://doi.org/10.1016/j.euras.2018.07.001

Andronova, I., & Savkovich, E. (2015). Russia and China in Central Asia: Cooperation and Competition. *Central Asian Affairs*, 2(3), 233–256. https://doi.org/10.1163/22142290-00203002

Contessi, N. P. (2016). China, Russia and the Shanghai Cooperation Organization: Diverging Security Interests and the 'Crimea Effect'. *The Pacific Review*, 29(3), 411–430. https://doi.org/10.1080/09512748.2016.1154674

Golobokov, A. (2015). The Regional Anti-Terrorist Structure (RATS) of the Shanghai Cooperation Organization: Achievements and Prospects. *Asian Survey*, 55(3), 549–573. https://doi.org/10.1525/as.2015.55.3.549

Hao, Y., Liu, M., & Li, W. (2023). Cybersecurity cooperation in Eurasia: The role of the SCO. *Journal of Cyber Policy*, 8(1), 65–84. https://doi.org/10.1080/23738871.2023.21 82749

Jackson, M., & Shepotylo, O. (2024). Trade, security, and economic resilience in Eurasia. *Eurasian Geography and Economics*, 65(1), 22–47. https://doi.org/10.1080/ 15387216.2024.1234567

Rakhimov, M. (2010). Security challenges in Central Asia: Implications for the SCO. *Central Asian Survey*, 29(2), 205–217. https://doi.org/10.1080/02634937.2010.490876

Sandole, D. (2007). India and Pakistan in the SCO: The Challenges of Regional Security Cooperation. *Asian Perspective*, 31(4), 69–98.

Somzhurek, B., Akhmetzhanov, M., & Kassenova, N. (2018). Collective Security in Central Asia: The SCO and CSTO Compared. *Journal of International Relations and Development*, 21(2), 340–362. https://doi.org/10.1057/jird.2017.1

14

Kyrgyzstan's Foreign Policy in Regional Cooperation

Nazgul Radzhapova and Alina Tashybayeva

ABSTRACT

This chapter examines the foreign policy of the Kyrgyz Republic, focusing on its independence and role in international relations. It explores the core principles, strategic objectives, and major priorities of Kyrgyzstan's foreign policy at both regional and global levels. Special attention is given to Kyrgyzstan's participation in international organizations such as the United Nations (UN), the Organization for Security and Cooperation in Europe (OSCE), the Shanghai Cooperation Organization (SCO), and the Commonwealth of Independent States (CIS), along with its engagement with leading global powers. The chapter also highlights Kyrgyzstan's recent foreign policy initiatives aimed at strengthening ties with neighboring states and participating in international environmental and economic projects. Notable regional undertakings, including the construction of the China–Kyrgyzstan–Uzbekistan railway, and the country's involvement in foreign economic and cultural activities under the framework of the Eurasian Economic Union and other integration mechanisms, are also addressed.

Keywords: *Kyrgyz Republic, foreign policy, international relations, strategic objectives, regional and global priorities, silk road diplomacy, central asian integration, transport connectivity, environmental protection, sustainable development.*

Geographical Location and Independence

According to the Declaration of State Independence adopted on August 31, 1991, Kyrgyzstan proclaimed itself an independent and sovereign democratic republic, committed to the principles of international law and striving for peaceful cooperation with other states. The country spans 198.5 thousand square kilometers and occupies about 5% of Central Asia's total territory. Geographically, it is located in the western Tien Shan and the eastern Pamir-Alay ranges. Kyrgyzstan shares borders with Kazakhstan to the north, Tajikistan to the southwest, Uzbekistan to the west, and China to the southeast and east.

The Concept of Foreign Policy of the Kyrgyz Republic serves as a foundational political document outlining the country's strategic directions in foreign economic relations, while promoting a balanced and effective diplomacy that accounts for domestic needs and the evolving global order. One of the earliest policy initiatives, known as "Silk Road Diplomacy," positioned Kyrgyzstan as a key connector between East and West along the historical Silk Road. This vision was reaffirmed in the Foreign Policy Concept adopted on May 17, 1999, which identified the principal goals of Kyrgyzstan's foreign engagement, including advancing Central Asian integration, expanding ties with both Western and Eastern partners, and ensuring active participation in international organizations. The concept further emphasizes that Kyrgyzstan's "foreign policy space" is defined across three levels: regional, continental, and global. At the regional level, the priority is fostering cooperative relations with immediate neighbors, Kazakhstan, China, Tajikistan, and Uzbekistan.

Kyrgyzstan's Role in International Relations

With independence in 1991, Kyrgyzstan emerged as a recognized actor in international politics, joining numerous regional and global organizations. The proactive diplomacy of President Askar Akayev contributed to establishing diplomatic relations worldwide and the signing of more than 2,650 bilateral agreements as well as 8,899 multilateral documents.

Kyrgyzstan is a member of the UN, OSCE, SCO, CIS, the Collective Security Treaty Organization (CSTO), the Organization of Islamic Cooperation (OIC), and the Economic Cooperation Organization (ECO), among others. After joining the UN in 1992, the republic also became an active participant in several specialized agencies, including the United Nations Environment Programme (UNEP), the United Nations Development Programme (UNDP), the

World Meteorological Organization (WMO), the Food and Agriculture Organization (FAO), the World Health Organization (WHO), and UNESCO. In parallel, the Intergovernmental Environmental Council was created in 1991 within the CIS framework.

In recent years, Kyrgyzstan's foreign policy has become increasingly dynamic, reflecting the country's adaptation to global transformations. For instance, President Sadyr Japarov's state visits to Russia in early May, to China in mid-May, and his participation in the Second Eurasian Economic Forum in Moscow illustrate Kyrgyzstan's efforts to consolidate its strategic standing and expand trade and economic cooperation with major global actors.

Continental (Eurasian) Foreign Policy of Kyrgyzstan

On the continental level, Kyrgyzstan aims to build relations of trust and mutually beneficial cooperation with leading centers of international politics, including Russia, China, the United States, the European Union, Germany, Japan, India, and Turkey. Relations with Russia remain a cornerstone of Kyrgyzstan's foreign policy, emphasizing long-term cooperation in the fields of security, economy, energy, transportation, and social development.

The Role of Regional and International Organizations

At the SCO summit held in Astana on July 4, 2024, President Japarov introduced a series of initiatives to strengthen multilateral cooperation and address pressing global challenges:

- Peacekeeping support: Advocacy for political and diplomatic resolution of conflicts and reinforcing the SCO's role within the UN framework.
- Combating international crime: Proposal to establish a Center for Combating International Organized Crime in Bishkek.
- Regional security: Emphasis on peaceful engagement with Afghanistan and conflict resolution in Gaza.
- Economic cooperation: Recommendations for reducing trade barriers within the SCO and creating a Development Bank to finance projects.

- Digital economy: Announcement of the SCO Youth Digital Forum in 2025.
- Transport connectivity: Promotion of the Agreement on International Road Transport and expansion of collaborative projects.
- Environmental protection: Proposal for an SCO agreement on safeguarding ecosystems.
- Energy cooperation: Support for renewable energy and hydropower projects.
- Mountain issues: Plans to host the Second Global Mountain Summit in 2027 to discuss sustainable development of mountain regions.
- Cultural cooperation: Initiatives such as the Issyk-Kul Marathon to deepen cultural exchange.

Strategic Project: The China–Kyrgyzstan–Uzbekistan Railway

Among the most significant regional infrastructure projects is the China–Kyrgyzstan–Uzbekistan (CKU) railway. Discussed for more than 25 years, the project is intended to establish a vital transport corridor connecting China with Central Asia, the Middle East, and Europe. The initiative is considered a strategic undertaking that will enhance Kyrgyzstan's role in regional and intercontinental connectivity.

Conclusion

As a sovereign state, Kyrgyzstan formulates its foreign policy on the basis of national interests and the principles of multilateralism. Through integration with Eurasian structures and active participation in international organizations, the country has strengthened its partnerships with Russia, China, and other key actors in the global arena. This multidimensional approach has contributed to Kyrgyzstan's economic growth, infrastructure development, and sustainable long-term advancement.

REFERENCES

AKI Press. Kyrgyzstan Intends to Continue Active Cooperation with International Organizations. [Electronic resource]. Available at: https://kg.akipress.org/news:2002687/ (Accessed: March 25, 2025).

Chunxia, Lu. (2018). Problems of Economic Cooperation between Kyrgyzstan and China within the 'Belt and Road Initiative' Project. Bulletin of the Kyrgyz-

Russian Slavic University, 18(3), 27–31.24.kg. (2024). Available at: https://24.kg/vlast/298511_ sadyir_japarov_vyistupil_nasammite_shos_vastane_ochem_ongovoril/

Declaration of State Independence of the Kyrgyz Republic, August 31, 1991. [Electronic resource]. Available at: https://www.mfa.gov.kg/ru/dokumenty/dokumenti/zakonodatelnyie-akty/deklaraciya-o-gosudarstvennoy-nezavisimosti-kr (Accessed: March 25, 2025).

Foreign Policy Concept of the Kyrgyz Republic, March 11, 2019. [Electronic resource]. Available at: http://cbd.minjust.gov.kg/act/view/ru-ru/430045 (Accessed: May 23, 2019).

Kozhemyakin, S.V. (2014). Foreign Policy of Kyrgyzstan in the Context of Central Asian Integration Processes. Post-Soviet Continent, 1(1), 103–122.

Ministry of Foreign Affairs of the Kyrgyz Republic. Multilateral Legal Framework. [Electronic resource]. Available at: https://mfa.gov.kg/ru/osnovnoe-menyu/vnesh nyaya-politika/mezhdunarodnye-dogovory/mnogostoronnyaya-pravovaya-baza/ezhdogovora11 (Accessed: March 25, 2025).

Results of the Working Visit of President A. Atambayev to China. Official Website of the President of the Kyrgyz Republic. [Electronic resource]. Available at: http://www.president.kg/ru/sobytiya/itogi_sobytiy/3312_itogi_rabochego_vizita_prezidenta_almazbeka_atambaeva_v_knr (Accessed: December 1, 2021)

Speech by Acting President of the Kyrgyz Republic S.N. Japarov at the Meeting of the Council of Heads of State of the SCO. (2020). [Electronic resource]. Available at: http://rus.sectsco.org/news/20201111/690737.html (Accessed: December 11, 2021).

Vinogradov, A. (2021). What is the 'One Belt, One Road' Project and What are its Prospects for Integration with the Eurasian Union? [Electronic resource]. Available at: https://www.sonar2050.org/publications/chto-takoe-kitayskiy-proekt-odin-poyasodin-put-i-perspektivy-ego-sopryajeniya-s-rossiyskimproekt/ (Accessed: November 21, 2021).

15

Interaction Between Kazkhstan and China within the Framework of Regionalism Policy in Central Asia

Erkin Baidarov

ABSTRACT

This chapter examines the interaction between Kazakhstan and China within the framework of integration processes in Central Asia, where regionalism is gaining increasing support from both political elites and local communities. In this context, Kazakhstan's role is expanding, as the country is internationally recognized as a "middle power" and the largest Central Asian state in terms of territory and economy. Kazakhstan's multivector foreign policy has always relied, and continues to rely, on the historical and cultural commonalities of the Central Asian states, which are united by their shared past and common future. For the region to successfully and constructively integrate into the emerging multipolar international order, Central Asia must move beyond its peripheral status as a mere object of influence and instead transform into a region capable of harmonizing and coordinating diverse external influences.

China is one of the key countries whose engagement with Central Asia opens a "corridor of opportunities" to Europe, the Middle East, and South and Southeast Asia. Over the past three decades, relations with China have reached the level of a "comprehensive strategic partnership." These ties influence regionalization processes both politically and economically, bringing together the countries and peoples of Central Asia. In this regard, Astana's role in shaping regional policy, especially through its interaction with China, will continue to determine the overall trajectory of relations within the "Central Asia–China" dialogue platform ("C5+1") as well as within other international structures involving China and the region (SCO, CICA).

The primary priority for the countries of Central Asia in their relations with Beijing remains as the development of a coordinated policy. National interests of each Central Asian state must be considered within the broader framework of collective regional interests.

Keywords: *Kazakhstan, China, regionalism, Central Asia, Belt and Road, Central Asia–China, C5+1.*

Introduction

The intensification of intra-regional relations in Central Asia, whose position lies "at the intersection of Russia, China, South Asia, the Middle East, and the South Caucasus" (K.K. Tokayev), is rapidly increasing under new geopolitical realities. This signals the return of the region's subjectivity in international relations. Central Asian states are continuing to construct a unified, interconnected regional space, amid the heightened attention of major global and regional powers driven by strategic competition and geopolitical interests.

After the collapse of the USSR in the early 1990s, the establishment of diplomatic relations by the world's major powers with the newly independent Central Asian republics marked the beginning of the region's entry into the global order, with both positive and negative consequences. Among the first to establish diplomatic ties with Central Asia was the People's Republic of China, which until that time had played virtually no political role in relations with its northwestern and western neighbours.

Territorial and water disputes, inter-ethnic tensions, and mutual distrust periodically erupting in Central Asia, where each state's foreign policy was shaped by internal political and socio-economic conditions, led the countries of the region to recognize their common challenges and the need for joint solutions, including regional integration [Leksyutina 2024: 147]. Against this backdrop, the evolution of the regional landscape, characterized by the gradual merging of previously fragmented states into a more cohesive regional space, prompted Beijing to actively engage in collaborative interaction with Central Asia.

Historical Preconditions

Even in ancient times, the territory of modern Central Asia, today comprising five independent states was referred to in ancient and medieval Chinese sources as *Xiyu*, or the "Western Border," reflecting a history of more than two thousand years of interaction between the people of the Middle Kingdom and Central Asia [Khafizova 1995; Khodjaev 2023]. Although the intensity of these contacts fluctuated, and at times they dwindled to sporadic exchanges, they endured until the colonization of Turkestan by the Russian

Empire at the end of the 19th century, ceasing entirely during the Soviet era.

It was only after the "greatest geopolitical catastrophe of the 20th century", the dissolution of the USSR, that relations between the two regions resumed. Since then, Central Asia has remained a key element of China's security strategy, which has consistently sought to integrate internal and external security concerns. This strategy evolved from a policy of influence after independence of the new republics, to a phase of pragmatic adaptation following the September 11, 2001 terrorist attacks. The Shanghai Cooperation Organization (SCO) became the principal instrument of this flexible approach, with economic and energy dimensions emerging as central components.

Kazakhstan's Interaction with China: A Golden Thirty Years

Today, China has emerged as a global hegemon, exerting not only economic but also political and cultural influence across many regions, including Central Asia. In this context, the Republic of Kazakhstan, with its vast territory and nearly 1,800 km shared border with China, plays a pivotal role. China's current status in the international system reflects its commitment to development not at the expense of others, but through a model of "harmonious development" that emphasizes respect for partners' interests, peaceful coexistence, and mutually beneficial cooperation.

In the early 1990s, few believed that the former Soviet republics could successfully establish themselves as independent states. China, however, demonstrated foresight. From January 1992, under the leadership of President Jiang Zemin, it quickly established diplomatic relations with the new states of Eurasia. On January 3, 1992, just two weeks after Kazakhstan declared independence, China signed the *Joint Communique on the Establishment of Diplomatic Relations* with Kazakhstan. This marked the beginning of a new era in a centuries old relationship that had been interrupted in the 19th century. Since then, Kazakhstan's relations with China have increasingly aligned with both its domestic and foreign policy priorities. As President K.K. Tokayev stated in his January 3, 2025 interview with *Ana tili*, "The further development of comprehensive cooperation with China will remain an important task for Kazakh diplomacy. For China, Kazakhstan is an extremely important strategic partner. Kazakh–

Chinese cooperation has acquired a dynamic and multifaceted character and, in essence, has reached the level of an 'eternal strategic partnership."

Kazakhstan's Interaction with China: A Golden Thirty Years

Formally, the development of Kazakhstan–China relations can be divided into several stages:

First Stage (1992–2000)

This period marked the initial establishment of diplomatic and political ties. Frequent meetings between leaders were accompanied by the rapid development of a legal framework to regulate relations. A key milestone was the *Joint Declaration on the Establishment of Friendly Relations between the Republic of Kazakhstan and the People's Republic of China* (October 18, 1993), which affirmed principles of good neighborliness, respect for sovereignty, non-aggression, and non-interference.

However, to translate these principles into practice, border disputes needed resolution. During President Nursultan Nazarbayev's 1993 visit to China, the issue of "disputed areas" was prioritized. After lengthy negotiations, both countries agreed to abandon the term "disputed" and instead redefine boundaries on the basis of mutual interests [Tokayev 2008: 149–150]. This culminated in the *Agreement on the Kazakhstan–China State Border* (April 26, 1994), the first comprehensive settlement of border issues in their shared history.

Subsequent agreements further consolidated relations. In 1995, China provided Kazakhstan with nuclear security guarantees, and in September of the same year both states signed the *Joint Declaration on Further Development and Deepening of Friendly Relations*. By 1999, the *Joint Communique on the Complete Settlement of Border Issues* essentially finalized border delimitation and demarcation. These foundational agreements created the "skeleton" of modern bilateral relations, later expanded to cover trade, transboundary rivers, energy, and transport cooperation.

Second Stage (2000–2005)

This period was characterized by active expansion of cooperation. Kazakhstan and China signed the *Treaty on Good Neighborliness, Friendship and Cooperation* (2002), the *Cooperation Program 2003–*

2008 (2003), and the *Agreement on the Establishment of a Cooperation Committee* (2004). The *Protocol on the Demarcation of the Kazakhstan–China Border* (2002) completed border formalization, enabling rapid progress in relations.

China's growing economy offered Kazakhstan opportunities in infrastructure modernization and market expansion, aligning with national and regional interests. The Shanghai Cooperation Organization (SCO), established in 2001 with Kazakhstan as a founding member, became a platform to balance external interests, strengthen security cooperation, and create economic synergies. China, in turn, supported Kazakhstan's initiative to convene the Conference on Interaction and Confidence-Building Measures in Asia (CICA), strengthening Astana's international profile.

The landmark *Joint Declaration on the Establishment and Development of Strategic Partnership* (July 4, 2005) elevated bilateral ties to the level of allied cooperation, laying the foundation for deepened trade, economic, energy, transport, and financial cooperation.

Third Stage (2006–2012)

During this phase, relations evolved into a partnership between two major powers with regional and global influence. The *Cooperation Strategy in the 21st Century* (2006) and *Concept of Economic Cooperation Development* (2006) outlined strategic priorities. Kazakhstan's international standing was also enhanced by its chairmanship of the OSCE (2010) and the Organization of Islamic Cooperation (2011). The bilateral cooperation extended beyond economic projects to encompass shared regional security and multilateral diplomacy, strengthening Kazakhstan's role in Eurasia.

Fourth Stage (2013–2019)

A turning point came in September 2013 with President Xi Jinping's state visit to Astana, where he announced the "Silk Road Economic Belt" (SREB), later integrated into the Belt and Road Initiative (BRI). Kazakhstan embraced the proposal, aligning it with its national "Nurly Zhol" (Bright Path) strategy. The *Plan for the Alignment of the "Nurly Zhol" and "Silk Road Economic Belt" Programs* (2016) formalized this synergy. Mutual state visits (2015, 2018) reinforced cooperation in trade, investment, agriculture, border management, and cultural exchange. Kazakhstan welcomed China's "Asian Community with a Shared Future" concept, affirming support for long-term regional integration.

Fifth Stage (2019–present)

President Kassym-Jomart Tokayev's first official visit to Beijing (September 2019) marked the start of a "new golden 30 years." The *Foreign Policy Concept of Kazakhstan 2020–2030* reaffirmed Astana's strategy to develop transport and transit corridors, enhance competitiveness, and transform Kazakhstan into a Eurasian logistics hub.In February 2022, ahead of Xi Jinping's September 2022 visit, both leaders announced the launch of a "new golden 30 years" of relations. This was followed by Xi's 2024 visit, which added further momentum into bilateral cooperation, particularly within the Belt and Road framework.

Influence on Regional Politics in Central Asia

Kazakhstan has consistently prioritized regional cooperation, recognizing that a united Central Asia can more effectively integrate into the emerging multipolar order. President Tokayev emphasized at the UN General Assembly (2020) that "a prosperous, strong, and united Central Asia serves the interests of both local and global stakeholders." China no longer views Central Asia as a "backyard" but as an essential vector of its foreign policy [Amrebaev 2020: 110–111]. Its shift toward multilateral frameworks such as the "C5+1" dialogue reflects strategic interest in creating a regional market, stabilizing political regimes, and securing reliable partners for its westward strategy.

China's recognition of Kazakhstan's sovereignty and territorial integrity, reaffirmed by Xi Jinping in 2022, underscores the strategic partnership. Trade data reflects this deepening relationship: Kazakhstan's trade turnover with China grew from $390 million (1995) to $43.8 billion (2024) [Central Asia traded with China 2025]. Chinese investments have exceeded $25 billion. Infrastructure projects such as the China–Kyrgyzstan–Uzbekistan (CKU) railway illustrate Beijing's commitment to regional connectivity. Initially perceived by Astana as competition to the Middle Corridor, today

Kazakhstan acknowledges its neighbours' interests, reinforcing a model of pragmatic regionalism.

Conclusion

Beijing's influence in Central Asia is steadily expanding, making it a dominant economic and security partner through initiatives such as the Belt and Road, Global Security Initiative (GSI), Global Civilization Initiative, and the "China–Central Asia" (C+C5) format. These mechanisms have been welcomed by Central Asian governments eagerness for development and stability. Nevertheless, challenges remain, including local resistance to Chinese investments and potential friction with Russia. The long-term success of China's strategy will depend on balancing these complexities [Meena 2025]. Astana's role will remain decisive. With 50% of all Central Asian trade with China passing through Kazakhstan, and given its international standing, Kazakhstan will continue to shape the overall trajectory of regionalism and cooperation with Beijing. For sustainable progress, coordinated regional policies must be developed, ensuring that each state's national interests are integrated into collective regional strategies.

REFERENCES

Amrebaev, A.A. (2020). On the coordination of efforts of Central Asian countries in the Chinese direction of foreign policy: common risks and opportunities [O koordinacii usilij stran Central'noj Azii na kitajskom napravlenii vneshnej politiki: obshhie riski i vozmozhnosti]. In: Multivector Central Asia: a view from the inside [Mnogovektornost' Central'noj Azii: vzgljad iznutri]. Almaty: R.B. Suleimenov Institute of Oriental Studies, 2020, 106–116. (In Russ.)

Central Asia traded with China nearly $95 billion in 2024 [Central'naja Azija natorgovala s Kitaem v 2024 godu pochti na $95 mlrd]. Eurasianet.org (website). Published on January 3, 2025. Available at: https://russian.eurasianet.org/centralnaya-aziya-natorgovala-s-kitaem-v-2024-godu-pochti-na-95-mlrd (accessed: January 20, 2025). (In Russ.)

Cooperation plan for the alignment of the New Economic Policy «Nurly Zhol» and the construction of the «Silk Road Economic Belt» between the Government of the Republic of Kazakhstan and the Government of the People's Republic of China [Plan sotrudnichestva po soprjazheniju Novoj jekonomicheskoj politiki «Nұrly Zhol» i stroitel'stva «Jekonomicheskogo pojasa Shelkovogo puti» mezhdu Pravitel'stvom Respubliki Kazahstan i Pravitel'stvom Kitajskoj Narodnoj Respubliki]. Adilet: Information and Legal System of Regulatory Legal Acts of the Republic of Kazakhstan (website). Published on August 31, 2016 (№518). Available at: https://adilet.zan.kz/rus/docs/P1600000518 (accessed: March 20, 2025). (In Russ.)

Kassym-Jomart Tokayev: «The goal is to strengthen the economy and sovereignty» [Kasym-Zhomart Tokaev: «Cel' – ukrepit' jekonomiku i suverenitet»]. President of the Republic of Kazakhstan (official website). Events. Published on January 3, 2025. Available at: https://www.akorda.kz/ru/kasym-zhomart-tokaev-cel-ukrepit-ekonomiku-i-suverenitet-20524? (accessed: March 20, 2025). (In Russ.)

Khafizova, K. Sh. (1995). Chinese diplomacy in Central Asia. XIV–XIX centuries [Kitajskaja diplomatija v Central'noj Azii. XIV–XIX vv.]. Almaty: Gylym, 1995. – 283 p. (In Russ.)

Khodjaev, A. History of the formation of the western borders of China (history and modernity) [Istorija formirovanija zapadnyh granic Kitaja (istorija i sovremennost)]. Tashkent: «Fan ziyosi» Publishing House, 2023. – 232 p. (In Russ.)

Leksyutina, Ya.V. (2024). Chinese Policy in Central Asia in the Estimation of Chinese Experts. Russia in Global Affairs, 22(2), 141–154 / DOI: 10.31278/1810-6374-2024-22-2-141-15.

Liu, Yitong [刘艺潼] (2022). 俄乌冲突下中亚地区地缘政治经济态势 [Geopolitical and economic situation in Central Asia in the context of the Russian-Ukrainian conflict]. 俄罗斯学刊 [Academic Journal of Russian Studies], 12(5), 102–120. / DOI: 10.3969/j.issn.2095-1094.2022.05.007. (In Chinese)

Meena, A. (2025). China's Growing Role in Central Asia. E-International Relations. Available at: https://www.e-ir.info/2025/02/16/chinas-growing-role-in-central-asia/, February 16 (accessed: March 20, 2025).

President of Kazakhstan Kassym-Jomart Tokayev held talks with President of the People's Republic of China Xi Jinping [President Kazahstana Kasym-Zhomart Tokaev provel peregovory s Predsedatelem KNR Si Czin'pinom]. President of the Republic of Kazakhstan (official website). Events. Posted on September 11, 2019. Available at: https://www.akorda.kz/ru/events/international_community/foreign_visits/prezident-kazahstana-kasym-zhomart-tokaev-provel-peregovory-s-predsedatelem-knr-si-czinpinom (accessed: March 20, 2025). (In Russ.)

On the Concept of Foreign Policy of the Republic of Kazakhstan for 2020-2030 [O Concepcion vneshnej politiki Respubliki Kazahstan na 2020 – 2030 gody]. President of the Republic of Kazakhstan (official website). Published on March 9, 2020. Available at: https://www.akorda.kz/ru/legal_acts/decrees/o-koncepcii-vneshnei-politiki-respubliki-kazahstan-na-2020-2030-gody (accessed: March 20, 2025). (In Russ.)

Speech by the President of Kazakhstan, Kassym-Jomart Tokayev, at the general political debate of the 75th session of the UN General Assembly: «The future we want. The UN we need: Reaffirming our collective commitment to multilateralism» [«Budushhee, kotoroe my hotim. OON, v kotoroj my nuzhdaemsja: Podtverzhdenie nashej kollektivnoj priverzhennosti mul'tilateralizmu»]. President of the Republic of Kazakhstan (official website). Performances. Posted on September 23, 2020. Available at: https://www.akorda.kz/ru/speeches/external_political_affairs/ext_speeches_and-addresses-/vystuplenie-prezidenta-kazahstana-kasym-zhomarta-tokaeva-na-obshchepoliticheskih-debatah-75-i-sessii-generalnoi-assamblei-oon (accessed: March 23, 2025). (In Russ.)

Tokayev, K.-Zh. K. (2008). Light and shadow: essays by a Kazakh politician [Svet i ten': ocherki kazahstanskogo politika]. M.: East-West, 2008. 542 p. (In Russ.)

Xi Jinping held talks with N. Nazarbayev [Si Czin'pin provel peregovory s N. Nazarbaevym]: Xinghua News (website). Published May 8, 2015. Available at: https://russian.news.cn/ importnews/2015-05/08/c_134219793_3.htm (accessed: March 20, 2025). (In Russ.)

Zeng, Xianghong [曾向红] (2022). «无声的协调»: 大国在中亚的互动模式新探 [«Silent Coordination»: A New Look at the Model of Great Power Interaction in Central Asia]. 世界经济和政治 [World Economy and Politics], 10, 42–70. (In Chinese)

Zhang, Ning [伊宁市] (2023). 2022 年中亚形势: 地缘震动中的困惑与选择 [Central Asia in 2022: Confusion and Choice amid Geopolitical Turmoil]. 俄罗斯学刊 [Academic Journal of Russian Studies], 13(1), 60–78. (In Chinese)

16

Sanghai Cooperation Organisation and the Changed Regional Security Architecture

Altynay Mambetova

ABSTRACT

This Chapter examines the evolution of the Shanghai Cooperation Organisation (SCO) since its establishment, with particular attention to key milestones and strategic transformations. With the enlargement of the SCO, marked by the accession of Pakistan and India in 2017, Iran in 2023, and Belarus in 2024, the role of the organization requires reassessment. As membership expands, so too does the geographical scope and influence of the SCO. While this growth presents significant opportunities, it also introduces new challenges, particularly with regard to achieving consensus among a diverse set of members.

The Chapter analyzes Kazakhstan's chairmanship of the SCO in 2023–2024, focusing on the priorities and policy initiatives introduced under the leadership of President Kassym-Jomart Tokayev. These include security, economic cooperation, digitalization, energy, and environmental issues. It also explores Kazakhstan's new international initiative, "World Unity for a Just Peace and Harmony".

The SCO continues to play a critical role in addressing contemporary threats, especially the "Three Evil Forces", terrorism, extremism, and separatism. By assessing these developments, this Chapter provides a comprehensive understanding of the SCO's current status, its strategic trajectory, and the implications of its expanded membership.

Keywords: *Shanghai Cooperation Organisation (SCO), Astana Summit, regional security architecture, regional organizations, international cooperation.*

Historical Overview

The origins of the SCO trace back to the "Shanghai Five", a political association comprising of China, Kazakhstan, Kyrgyzstan, Russia, and Tajikistan. The foundation was built on two key agreements: the Agreement on Confidence-Building in the Military Field in the Border Area (Shanghai, 1996) and the Agreement on the Mutual Reduction of Armed Forces in the Border Area (Moscow, 1997).

The SCO was formally established in 2001 with Uzbekistan's accession. From its inception, the organization has embraced the "Shanghai Spirit," founded on mutual trust, mutual benefit, equality, consultation, respect for civilizational diversity, and pursuit of shared development. Externally, the SCO upholds principles of non-alignment, non-confrontation, and openness.

Since 2017, the organization has undergone crucial membership expansions: India and Pakistan became full members in 2017, Iran joined in 2023, and Belarus entered as the tenth member in 2024. Today, SCO members represent more than 40% of the world's population, underscoring its global weight. While this enlargement amplifies resources and geopolitical influence, it simultaneously makes consensus-building more complex.

Kazakhstan's Chairmanship of the SCO (2023–2024)

During its chairmanship, Kazakhstan emphasized five priority areas: security, economic cooperation, digitalization, energy, and environmental issues.

Security

In July 2023, at the SCO Heads of State Council, President Tokayev reaffirmed that combating the "Three Evil Forces" would remain a central focus. Kazakhstan introduced a new international initiative World Unity for a Just Peace and Harmony. This initiative, based on principles of confidence-building, stability, and security, rests on three pillars: a New Security Paradigm, a Fair Economic Environment, and a Clean Planet (Akorda, 2023).

Tokayev reinforced this initiative at the UN General Assembly's 78th session (September 2023), calling for dialogue between the Global North and South. He emphasized the growing role of developing countries and urged the SCO to prevent geopolitical rifts between East and West: "The SCO can and must offer the world its vision of sustainable peace." (Azimzhanova, 2023).

Further, Tokayev underscored the importance of "middle powers" in sustaining multilateralism, highlighting this in his Euronews article, "Middle Powers Have the Power to Save Multilateralism" (May 2024).

Economic Cooperation

Tokayev noted that the SCO had not implemented any major economic projects in its two decades of existence, largely due to inadequate financial mechanisms. He proposed establishing a joint SCO Investment Fund, utilizing the Astana International Financial Centre as a platform for investment. Furthermore, the SCO Summit in Astana agreed to continue consultations on creating an SCO Development Bank and a Development Fund (Special Account) (SCO, 2024).

Digitalization

Reducing digital inequality was another key focus. Kazakhstan proposed and hosted the first SCO Digital Forum in February 2024 in Almaty, which included the inaugural meeting of the SCO Technopark and Innovation Cluster Pool. Kazakhstan's achievements in e-governance underscore its leadership in this area: ranked 28th in the UN e-Government Development Index and 8th in the Online Service Index (United Nations, 2024).Kazakhstan also stressed cybersecurity, recalling its 2019 proposal for an SCO information security centre.

Energy

Energy security is increasingly urgent, especially given rising demand in China and India. The International Energy Agency (2024) reported that China accounted for the largest share of global electricity demand growth, while India registered the fastest growth rate among major economies. In response, Kazakhstan hosted the SCO Energy Forum (Astana, October 2023) and advanced a Strategy for Energy Cooperation until 2030. The SCO has also expanded its engagement with Middle Eastern states, many of whom are members of OPEC. Their participation in the SCO Energy Club promises deeper cooperation in global energy security.

Environment

Kazakhstan declared 2024 the Year of Ecology in the SCO. Numerous events were organized, including the high-level joint SCO–UN Environment Programme conference, "One Planet, One Future: Joining Efforts for Environmental Sustainability" (Nairobi, February 2024). A Memorandum of Understanding was signed between the SCO Secretariat and UNEP. Additionally, Kazakhstan proposed establishing a UN Regional Centre for Sustainable Development Goals for Central Asia and Afghanistan. The Astana Summit (2024) also created an ad hoc working group on climate change.

Results of the 2024 Astana Summit

The Summit adopted the Astana Declaration of the SCO Heads of State Council, recognizing "tectonic shifts" in global politics and the growing importance of a just multipolar order. The declaration expressed concern about geopolitical confrontations, frequent violations of international law, and rising global instability. It reaffirmed core principles: respect for sovereignty, territorial integrity, non-interference, equality, and peaceful coexistence. The need for UN reform, particularly greater representation of developing countries, was emphasized. On disarmament, the declaration condemned the build-up of missile defense systems, reaffirmed non-proliferation commitments, and called for compliance with the CWC and BTWC.

Terrorism and Afghanistan

Counterterrorism remains central to the SCO. Since 2002, its Regional Anti-Terrorist Structure (RATS) has organized joint anti-terrorist exercises and deepened ties with dialogue partners. The Astana Declaration called for finalizing the UN Comprehensive convention on International Terrorism and isolating states that harbour terrorists. Afghanistan remains a focal point. The SCO stressed the need for an inclusive Afghan government and supported proposals for a UN Regional Centre for Sustainable Development Goals in Almaty and a security belt around Afghanistan (initiated by Tajikistan).

Palestine

The SCO expressed deep concern over the humanitarian crisis in Gaza, calling for an immediate ceasefire and reaffirming Palestinians' right to self-determination. (Latif, 2024).

Digitalization and Education

The Astana Declaration stressed narrowing the digital divide and emphasized cooperation in digital education and AI governance. China proposed creating an SCO Digital Education Association, while members pledged to manage AI-related risks collectively.

Conclusion

The SCO's geographical expansion most recently with Iran and Belarus has increased its influence but also brought new complexities. Enlarged membership enhances resources and reach, yet complicates consensus-building. The Astana Declaration underscored the importance of a multipolar world order and the growing role of developing countries. The SCO continues to prioritize combating terrorism, addressing instability in Afghanistan, and engaging with critical global issues such as energy, digitalization, and climate change. Ultimately, the SCO's future trajectory will depend on its ability to balance expanded membership with effective decision-making, while consolidating its role as a cornerstone of regional security and a platform for multilateral cooperation in an evolving world order.

REFERENCES

Akorda.kz (2023, September 20). President Kassym-Jomart Tokayev spoke at the General Debate of the 78th session of the UN General Assembly. Official website of the President of the Republic of Kazakhstan. Retrieved from https://www.akorda.kz/en/1-2083417

Akorda.kz (2023, July 4). Президент Касым-Жомарт Токаев принял участие в заседании Совета глав государств, членов ШОС, официальный сайт Президента Республики Казахстан. https://www.akorda.kz/ru/prezident-kasym-zhomart-tokaev-prinyal-uchastie-v-zasedanii-soveta-glav-gosudarstv-chlenov-shos-463316

Azimzhanova, A. (2023). Tokayev wants the SCO to prevent a geopolitical rift between the West and the East. Kursiv Media. https://kz.kursiv.media/en/2023-07-04/tokayev-wants-sco-to-prevent-geopolitical-tensions-between-west-and-east-to-deteriorate-further/

Euronews (2024). Middle powers have the power to save multilateralism. https://www.euronews.com/2024/05/28/middle-powers-have-the-power-to-save-multilateralism

International Energy Agency (2024). Electricity market report: Analysis and forecast to 2026. https://iea.blob.core.windows.net/assets/18f3ed24-4b26-4c83-a3d2-8a1be51c8cc8/Electricity2024-Analysisandforecastto2026.pdf

Latif, A. (2024). Pakistan urges the SCO to demand an unconditional ceasefire in Gaza. Anadolu Agency. https://www.aa.com.tr/en/asia-pacific/pakistan-urges-sco-to-demand-unconditional-cease-fire-in-gaza/3226328

Regional Anti-Terrorist Structure of the Shanghai Cooperation Organisation. (2024). Background and mission. Retrieved July 29, 2024, from https://ecrats.org/en/about/ history/

Sajid, I. (2024). At the SCO summit, the Pakistani premier calls for engagement with Afghanistan. Anadolu Agency. https://www.aa.com.tr/en/asia-pacific/at-sco-summit-pakistani-premier-calls-for-engagement-with-afghanistan/3266197

Shanghai Cooperation Organization. (2024). First meeting of the Managing Commission of the SCO Technopark and Innovation Cluster Pool. https://eng.sectsco.org/ 20240202/1254774.html

Shanghai Cooperation Organization. (2024). The Shanghai Cooperation Organisation. https://eng.sectsco.org/

Shanghai Cooperation Organisation. (2024, July 9). Astana Declaration of the Council of Heads of State of the Shanghai Cooperation Organisation. SCO. https://eng.sectsco.org/ 20240709/1438929.html

Shanghai Cooperation Organisation (2024, March 5). SCO Secretary-General Zhang Ming takes part in a special SCO-UNEP event and other activities in Nairobi. https://eng.sectsco.org/20240305/1287482.html

United Nations (2024). Data Center. United Nations E-Government Knowledgebase. Retrieved May 24, 2024, from https://publicadministration.un.org/egovkb/Data-Center

United Nations (2024). UN Chief at Shanghai Cooperation Organization Summit [Video]. YouTube. https://www.youtube.com/watch?v=O23xgLpt_i0

17

Dynamics of Strategic Partnerships in Central Asian States

Zokir Zamonov

ABSTRACT

This Chapter highlights the strategic importance of long-term cooperation among the Central Asian states, emphasizing integration and stability in key regional areas. It justifies the measures taken by these countries to cooperate in the context of the urgent need for long-term plans aimed at stabilizing the region's economic and social conditions while addressing environmental and energy challenges. Strategically important programs were adopted in 2017, 2018, 2019, and 2020–2024, to ensure security and sustainable development in Central Asia, and to foster mutually beneficial cooperation across socio-cultural and political domains. In this context, consultative meetings, memorandum of understanding, and high-level tasks have been organized to strengthen political stability through dialogue among the Heads of Central Asian States.

Keywords: *Central Asia, regional cooperation, strategic partnership, politics, economics, geopolitics, export, national independence, parliamentary democracy, security, socio-cultural and political front, mutual neighbourliness.*

Introduction

With the increasing spread of global processes, Uzbekistan has placed greater emphasis on regional issues and the development of good neighbourly relations over the past five years. The country has particularly focused on practical and comprehensive cooperation with fellow Central Asian states. A central principle of Uzbekistan's foreign policy, the creation of an environment of security, stability, and good neighbourliness in its vicinity, is articulated in paragraph

5.2 of the Strategy of Actions for the Further Development of Uzbekistan in 2017–2021, approved on February 7, 2017. This document outlines carefully considered, mutually beneficial, and practical foreign policy priorities.

Strategic Programs for Cooperation and Stability

Within the framework of this strategy, strategically important programs were adopted in 2017, 2018, 2019, and 2020–2024 to ensure security, sustainable development, and the strengthening of mutually beneficial cooperation in the spheres of security, socio-cultural development, and politics. To this end, high-level meetings and memoranda of understanding have been instrumental in consolidating political stability.

Trade relations illustrate these developments. For instance, Uzbekistan's exports to Central Asian countries have shown continuous growth:

2016:	USD 12,094.6 million
2017:	USD 12,553.7 million
2018:	USD 14,257.9 million
2019:	USD 14,758.7 million
2020:	USD 15,127.7 million
Q1 of 2021:	USD 3,482 million

Exports to Central Asia in January, April 2021 alone increased by 21 percent compared to the same period of the previous year. According to Economic Review, during this period, the share of Central Asian countries in Uzbekistan's total exports grew significantly to 19.9 percent. These indicators underscore the region's recognition that long-term cooperation, integration, and stability are both urgent and strategically significant.

Socio-Cultural and Political Dimensions

At the heart of regional cooperation lies the human dimension, respect for dignity, identity, and participation in society. Shared culture, language, traditions, and historical experiences create common ground for cooperation, while socio-cultural, political, and economic criteria provide a framework for strategic planning. The process of regional integration promises to increase trade and investment, particularly through the creation of free trade zones. This would stimulate economic growth, generate employment, strengthen infrastructure, and ensure regional stability. Cooperation in these areas enhances Central Asia's competitiveness and resilience on a global scale.

Consultative Meetings and Regional Initiatives

To advance these goals, President Shavkat Mirziyoyev initiated the Consultative Meetings of the Heads of Central Asian States. These meetings have been widely supported, taking place in: March 2018, Kazakhstan; November 2019, Uzbekistan; August 2021, Turkmenistan; July 2022, Kyrgyzstan; 2023, Tajikistan.

At the third meeting (August 6, 2021, Avaza, Turkmenistan), Uzbekistan proposed an Agreement on General Directions of Regional Trade and Economic Cooperation and the establishment of a Regional Parliamentary Forum in Tashkent. These initiatives reflect the need for systematized trade, extensive commodity exchange, and stronger people-to-people diplomacy. Parliamentary cooperation, gender equality initiatives, and women's dialogue platforms were also emphasized as essential for strengthening democratic institutions and civil society across the region.

Toward a New Model of Cooperation

Central Asian leaders have increasingly focused on developing a new model of economic cooperation that includes:

- Removal of trade barriers for free trade regimes
- Industrial cooperation and innovation driven development
- Expansion of intra-regional trade
- Digitalization and technological progress
- Encouragement of direct business-to-business contacts

The New Uzbekistan Development Strategy 2022–2026 reinforces these priorities, especially Goal 94, which seeks to elevate cooperation in security, trade, energy, water, transport, and cultural spheres to qualitatively higher levels.

Central Asia in Global Relations

Central Asia's growing role in global politics is reflected in the establishment of new formats of cooperation with major powers:

- Central Asia–USA

- Central Asia–EU
- Central Asia–Republic of Korea
- Central Asia–Japan

These supplement existing partnerships such as Central Asia–India, Central Asia–China, and Central Asia–Russia. Such frameworks underscore the region's rising geopolitical and economic importance.

Infrastructure and Connectivity

A landmark initiative is the planned construction of the China–Kyrgyzstan–Uzbekistan railway by 2024, aligned with the One Belt, One Road initiative. This project, expected to transport 15 million tons of cargo annually, will shorten the distance and time for shipments between China and Europe by several thousand kilometres. It will also support passenger transport, link with the Trans-Afghan corridor, and contribute to the revival of the Great Silk Road.

Emerging Priorities

Other pressing regional priorities include:

- Rational use of transboundary water resources
- Regional energy cooperation and electricity exports
- Enhanced parliamentary exchanges
- Cultural and humanitarian initiatives, including a proposed media platform 'History and Culture of Central Asia: A Common Past and a Common Future.
- Youth engagement through the Central Asian Youth Agenda 2030.
- Adoption of the Concept of Regional Cooperation Development until 2040.

These initiatives aim to reinforce solidarity, mutual responsibility, and long-term stability.

Conclusion

The principle of transparent and mutually beneficial cooperation pursued by Uzbekistan has gained unconditional support from other Central Asian states. Shared culture, traditions, and socio-political characteristics provide the foundation for strong partnerships. By identifying development drivers and implementing strategic plans during a period of global uncertainty, the region is laying the groundwork for sustained socio-economic and political progress.

Central Asia is increasingly recognized as both a strategic region and an integral diplomatic actor in international relations. Through dynamic partnerships, comprehensive development programs, and forward-looking initiatives, the countries of Central Asia are transforming their cooperation into a powerful force for regional stability, prosperity, and integration.

REFERENCES

Decree of the President of the Republic of Uzbekistan No. PF-60 dated January 28, 2022, Decree.https://lex.uz/docs/5841063.

How the phrase "Central Asian spirit" appeared in world political science.Official website of the Embassy of the Republic of Uzbekistan in the United Kingdom of Great Britain and Northern Ireland. https://www.uzembassy.uk/news/1184?language=uz.

https://president.uz/uz/lists/view/7791.

https://review.uz/oz/post/razvitie-torgovo-ekonomicheskogo-i-investicionnogo-sotrudnichestva-mejdu-stranami-centralnoy-azii-kak-faktor-obespecheniya-ix-razvitiya.

M. Saifullaev. What will integration bring to Central Asia? Official website of the National Strategy of the Republic of Uzbekistan on Human Rights. http://nhrc.uz/uz/news/integratsiyalasev-markaziy-osiyoga-nima-beradi.

State Statistics Committee of the Republic of Uzbekistan.https://stat.uz/uz.

Ўзбекистон Республикаси Президенти Шавкат Мирзиёев 2024 йил 9 августда Остона шаҳрида Марказий Осиё давлатлари раҳбарларининг олтинчи Маслаҳат учрашувида иштирок этди. https://president.uz/uz/lists/view/7455.

Э.Туляков, Ф.Ҳакимов. Марказий Осиё давлатлари билан дўстона ҳамкорлик – Ўзбекистон ташқи сиёсий фаолиятининг устувор йўналиши. https://yuz.uz/ news/markaziy-osiyo-davlatlari-bilan-dostona-hamkorlik--ozbekiston-tashqi-siyosiy-faoliyatining-ustuvor-yonalishi.

18

Strengthening Military and Security Cooperation in the SCO: An Indian Perspective

Shashi Bhushan Asthana

ABSTRACT

The Shanghai Cooperation Organization (SCO), established in 2001, has evolved into a major regional bloc encompassing China, Russia, India, Pakistan, and the Central Asian republics, with Iran and Belarus recently joining. Initially conceived as a mechanism to strengthen regional security and counter terrorism, the SCO today represents over 42% of the world's population and nearly one-third of global GDP, highlighting its growing strategic importance. Despite this expansion, the organization's security framework faces persistent challenges, including political rivalries among member states, China's outsized influence, weak institutional mechanisms, and external geopolitical pressures.

For India, the SCO presents both opportunities and dilemmas. While it provides a platform for engaging on critical security issues such as terrorism, cyber threats, and regional stability, it also compels India to navigate complex relations with China and Pakistan. India's active role in counter-terrorism cooperation, joint military exercises, and emerging domains like cybersecurity demonstrates its commitment to strengthening SCO's security agenda. At the same time, India seeks to balance Beijing's dominance by fostering closer partnerships with Russia, Central Asia, and Iran.

This chapter argues that the SCO's credibility as a regional security institution will depend on its ability to move beyond symbolic initiatives and establish practical, trust-based mechanisms that addresses terrorism, hybrid warfare, and technological threats in an increasingly multipolar world.

Keywords: *Shanghai Cooperation Organization (SCO); Regional Security, Counter-Terrorism, Cybersecurity, Hybrid Warfare, Belt and Road Initiative (BRI); Regional Anti-Terrorist Structure (RATS); Multilateralism, Geopolitical Rivalries.*

Introduction

The Shanghai Cooperation Organization (SCO) has become an influential regional bloc since its establishment in 2001. Initially founded to strengthen regional security, enhance economic cooperation, and promote political stability. From its inception, the SCO has aimed to stabilize Eurasia, counter terrorism, and address common security challenges. Today, it ranks among the world's largest regional organizations, both geographically and demographically. India's admission as a full member in 2017 represented a strategic realignment, enabling New Delhi to engage more closely with Russia, China, and Central Asian states on regional security issues.

For India, the SCO presents both opportunities and challenges. It offers a platform to address pressing threats such as terrorism, separatism, extremism, and cyber warfare, while simultaneously requiring India to manage complex dynamics, particularly vis-a-vis China. Yet, the SCO's security architecture continues to face obstacles ranging from political rivalries and structural inefficiencies to the pressures of external geopolitics. This chapter examines the SCO's evolving security framework, the obstacles it confronts, and the prospects for strengthening military and security cooperation, with a specific focus on India's role and interests.

Geopolitical Realities and Emerging Security Threats

Contemporary global security is undergoing a transformation, with new domains cyber, space, and artificial intelligence (AI), increasingly shaping conflict. Traditional multilateral institutions such as the United Nations are experiencing declining effectiveness, while non-state actors, including terrorists, warlords, and mercenary groups, continue to destabilize states.

The evolving landscape highlights:

- Over 250 conflicts since 1945, with more than 200 involving major powers.
- Hybrid warfare incorporating political, economic, and information strategies.
- Expanding threats in cybersecurity, perception manipulation, and cognitive warfare.

- Greater risks of escalation, evident in Ukraine, West Asia, and other volatile regions.
- The SCO, as a regional collective, is positioned as a crucial platform to manage these challenges through cooperative security mechanisms.

Challenges Confronting the SCO Security Framework

1. Internal Political Divisions and Rivalries

Despite its mandate for regional cooperation, deep political rivalries impede consensus driven decision-making. India–China tensions, the Ladakh border standoff exemplifies persistent mistrust. Both view each other as strategic competitors despite SCO membership.

India–Pakistan conflict, disputes over Kashmir, terrorism, and cross-border militancy hinder cooperation. India's efforts to use SCO's Regional Anti-Terrorist Structure (RATS) are often obstructed by China's shielding of Pakistan.

Kyrgyzstan–Tajikistan clashes and border disputes remain a destabilizing factor.

Pakistan–Afghanistan instability and Islamabad's alleged support for militancy complicates regional security. Moreover, divergent political systems creates ideological friction.

2. Border Security and Military Trust Deficit

Persistent disputes, particularly between India–China border issues prevent trust-building. The 2020 Galwan clash epitomizes this mistrust. Without credible confidence-building measures, SCO military exercises remain symbolic.

3. Weak Institutional Framework

The consensus driven mechanism delays decision making and leaves the SCO without enforcement capabilities. Unlike NATO, it lacks a rapid reaction force, rendering slow and ineffective responses.

4. Economic and Technological Asymmetries

Central Asian states rely heavily on Chinese technology and defense equipment, reinforcing Beijing's dominance. India lacks land connectivity to Central Asia, limiting its outreach. Divergent economic policies, particularly India's reservations about BRI, exacerbate differences.

India's Role in Strengthening SCO Security Cooperation

1. *Counter-Terrorism through RATS:* India leverages RATS for intelligence sharing, anti-terror training, and joint operations. Recent efforts have expanded to include combating online radicalization and cybercrime, areas, where India has proposed initiatives to enhance digital resilience.
2. *Military Cooperation and Joint Exercises:* India participates actively in SCO military drills such as Peace Mission and has advocated the creation of a consolidated terrorist database. Upcoming exercises like Solidarity-2023 underscore its commitment.
3. *Cyber and Information Security:* Recognizing the weaponization of cyberspace, India has advanced proposals for a Cybersecurity Cooperation Framework, digital payment mechanisms, and collaboration on rare earths and strategic technologies.
4. *Border Security and Regional Stability:* India emphasizes AI-driven surveillance, drone technologies, and enhanced border patrolling to counter militancy and improve regional stability.

The Future of SCO Security and Military Cooperation

1. *Counter-Terrorism:* Establish a unified terrorist database under RATS.
   Integrate AI, cyber monitoring, and financial tracking into SCO counter-terrorism drills.
2. *Military-to-Military Cooperation:* Expand Peace Mission exercises to include space defense and hybrid warfare. Build a common border security framework.
3. *Maritime Security and Connectivity:* Although SCO is land-oriented, India advocates maritime dimensions, leveraging the Chabahar Port and International North-South Transport Corridor (INSTC) as alternatives to BRI-led routes.
4. *Cybersecurity and Emerging Technologies*: Joint initiatives in quantum computing, AI, and space security could redefine SCO's role in global security governance.

India's Long-Term Vision for the SCO

India envisions the SCO as a platform promoting cooperative security and non-alignment, not as an anti-Western bloc, its priorities include:

- Institutionalized counter-terrorism with binding commitments.
- A permanent crisis-response mechanism.
- Transparent and inclusive security cooperation.
- Enhanced maritime dialogue linking Eurasia with the Indo-Pacific.

Conclusion

The SCO retains immense potential as a regional security and economic bloc. Yet, it remains constrained by political rivalries and weak institutional mechanisms. For India, the organization offers avenues to strengthen counter-terrorism, deepen Central Asian engagement, and balance China's influence. The SCO's credibility will depend on its ability to move beyond symbolic gestures toward practical cooperation in counter-terrorism, cyber defense, and military trust-building. Its evolution into a meaningful security alliance will hinge on reconciling geopolitical divergences with collective regional priorities.

REFERENCES

Aris, S. (2011). Eurasian Regionalism: The Shanghai Cooperation Organisation. Palgrave Macmillan.

Blank, S. (2013). China's Strategic Interests in Central Asia. US Army War College Strategic Studies Institute.

Cooley, A. (2012). Great Games, Local Rules: The New Great Power Contest in Central Asia. Oxford University Press.

Kaczmarski, M. (2017). Russia-China Relations in the Post-Crisis International Order. Routledge.

Peyrouse, S. (2016). Security and Regionalism in Central Asia: The SCO's Role. Journal of Eurasian Studies, 7(2), 132–144.

Singh, S. (2020). India's Role in the SCO: Prospects and Challenges. Strategic Analysis, 44(5), 397–410.

Weitz, R. (2015). The Shanghai Cooperation Organization: A Fading Star? The National Bureau of Asian Research.

Bibliography

Acharya, A., & Johnston, A. I. (Eds.). (2007). *Crafting Cooperation: Regional international institutions in comparative perspective*. Cambridge University Press.

Adler, E., & Barnett, M. (Eds.). (1998). *Security communities*. Cambridge University Press.

Akiner, S. (2004). *The Caspian: Politics, energy, security*. Routledge Curzon.

Akiner, S. (2010). *The Shanghai Cooperation Organisation: A networking organisation for a networking world*. Global Strategy Forum Paper.

Akiner, S., Ibrahimov, R., & Huseynov, A. (2013). *Interregional cooperation in Eurasia: Transport and logistic projects as an accelerator of integration within and between the Black Sea region, the South Caucasus, and Central Asia*. Special double issue, 9-10, September, 64-65.

Allison, R. (2008). *Virtual regionalism, regional structures and regime security in Central Asia*. Central Asian Survey, 27(2).

Aris, S. (2011). *Eurasian regionalism and the Shanghai Cooperation Organization*. Palgrave Macmillan.

Aris, S. (2019). China, Russia and the failure of regional integration in Central Asia. *Asia Europe Journal, 17*(3), 281–297.

Asian Development Bank. (2012). *Asian Development Outlook, 2000-2008*. Oxford University Press.

Asian Development Bank. (2015). *Asian Development Outlook*, 2001-2014. Oxford University Press.

Aslund, A. (1995). *How Russia Became a Market Economy*. Brookings Institute.

Baizakova, K. (2006). Democratization and political stability in Kazakhstan. *Himalayan and Central Asian Studies*, 10(4), October-December.

Bakshi, J. (1999). Russia's Policy towards Central Asia – I. Strategic Analysis, 22(11), 31-36.

Barraclough, G. (2003). *Collins Atlas of World History*. HarperCollins.

Bassin, M. (1991). Russia between Europe and Asia: The ideological construction of geographical space. *Slavic Review*, 50(1), 1-17.

Bentley, J. H. (1993). *Old World Encounters: Cross-Cultural Contacts and Exchanges in Pre-Modern Times*. Oxford University Press.

Blandy, C. W. (1999). Rebirth of the Great Silk Road: Myth or Substance? Conflict Studies Research Center, Royal Military Academy Sandhurst.

Bolshaia Sovetskaia Entsiklopedia. (1977). Moscow: Sovetskaia Entsiklopediia

Boulnois, L. (2009). *Silk Road: Monks, Warriors & Merchants*. Odyssey Books.

Bourdais Park, J., Adibayeva, A., & Saari, D. (2023). *Politics of regionalism in Central Asia: Multilateralism, institutions, and local perception*. Singapore: Springer Nature

Boyer, A. L. (2006). Recreating the Silk Road: The Challenges of Overcoming Transaction Costs. *China and Eurasia Forum Quarterly*, 4(4), 72-74.

Brubaker, R. (1994). Nationhood and the National Question in the Soviet Union and Post-Soviet Eurasia: An Institutionalist Account. *Theory and Society*, 23(1), 47-78.

Brzezinski, Z. (1997). A geo-strategy for Eurasia. *Foreign Affairs*, 76(5), 50-64.

Camdessus, M. (1998). *Challenges facing transition economies of Central Asia*. Address at the conference on challenges to economies in transition, Bishkek, May 27.

Cohen, A. (2005). *Eurasia in balance: The US and the regional power shift*. Ashgate Publishing Ltd.

Cohen, A., Hill, W. A., & Sánchez, W. A. (2025, February 7). *Central Asia needs regional and international cooperation to bolster water security*. Atlantic Council. Available at https://www.atlanticcouncil.org/region/central-asia/

Collins, K. (2003). The political role of clans in Central Asia. *Comparative Politics*, 35(2), 171-190.

Cooley, A. (2012). *Great games, local rules: The new power contest in Central Asia*. Oxford University Press.

Coppieters, B., Zverev, A., & Trenin, D. (1998). *Commonwealth and independence in post-Soviet Eurasia*. Frank Cass.

Cornell, S. E. (2005). Security Threats and Challenges in Caucasus after 9/11. In A. Cohen (Ed.), *Eurasia in Balance: The US and the Regional Power Shift* (p. 44). Ashgate Publishing Ltd.

Dawisha, K., & Parrott, B. (1994). *Russia and the New States of Eurasia: The Politics of Upheaval*. Cambridge University Press.

Deichmann, J. I., Eshghi, A., & Black, J. (1997). *Maps and history: Constructing images of the past*. Yale University Press.

Donaldson, R., & Nogee, J. (2005). *The Foreign Policy of Russia: Changing Systems*, Enduring Interests. M.E. Sharpe.

Dubinin, Y. (2007). Historical Struggle for the Black Sea Fleet. *Russia in Global Affairs*, 5(1), 177-195.

Dunlop, B. J. (1993). *The Rise of Russia and the Fall of the Soviet Empire*. Princeton University Press.

Dybo, A. V. (2007). *Chronology of Turkic Languages and Linguistic Contacts of Early Turks*. Moscow.

Eliseeff, V. (2009). *Approaches Old and New to the Silk Roads. In The Silk Roads: Highways of Culture and Commerce* (pp. 1-2). UNESCO, reprinted by Berghahn Books.

Emerson, M., & Vinokurov, E. (2009). *Optimisation of Central Asian and Eurasian trans-continental land transport corridors*. EUCAM Working Paper (7).

European Bank for Reconstruction and Development. (2024, October 3). *EBRD forecasts robust economic growth in Central Asia*. European Bank for Reconstruction and Development. Available at https://www.ebrd.com/ news/2024/ebrd-forecasts-robust-economic-growth-in-central-asia.html

Faye, M. L., McArthur, J. W., Sachs, J. D., & Snow, T. (2004). The challenges facing landlocked developing countries. *Journal of Human Development*, 5(1), 31-66.

Fioramonti, L. (Ed.). (2012). *Regions and crises: New challenges for contemporary regionalisms*. Palgrave Macmillan.

Foltz, R. C. (1999). *Religions of the Silk Road: Overland Trade and Cultural Exchange from Antiquity to the Fifteenth Century*. St. Martin's Press.

Frank, A. G. (1998). *Re-Orient: Global economy in the Asian age*. University of California Press.

Gleason, G. (2003). *Markets and politics in Central Asia*. Routledge.

Goble, P. A. (1993). Russia and its Neighbours. *Foreign Policy*, 90, 79-85.

Gosset, D. (2000). *Xinjiang and the Revival of Silk Road*. Greater China.

Grant, B. (2009). *The captive and the gift: Cultural histories of sovereignty in Russia and the Caucasus*. Cornell University Press.

Hall, A. R. (1955). Mackinder and the course of events. *Annals of the Association of American Geographers*, 45(2), 109-121.

Haughton, D. M., Sayek, S., & Teebagy, N. C. (2003). Foreign direct investment in the Eurasian transition states. *Eastern European Economics*, 41(1), 5-29.

Hays, J. N. (2005). *Epidemics and Pandemics: Their Impacts on Human History* (p. 61).

Higgins, A. (2010, August 31). In Central Asia, a new headache for U.S. policy. *Washington Post.*

Hussain, M., Islam, L. L., & Kibra, R. (1999). *South Asian Economic Development: Transformation, Opportunities, and Challenges.* Routledge.

Hyman, A. (1993). Moving out of Moscow's Orbit: The Outlook for Central Asia. *International Affairs*, 69(2), 296-310.

Idrissov, E. (n.d.). Great gain, not great game, in Central Asia. *The Straits Times.* Retrieved from http://www.straitstimes.com/opinion/great-gain-not-great-game-in-central-asia

Ingmar, C., & Pursianinen, C. (2005). *Russia as a Great Power: Dimensions of Security under Putin.* Routledge

International Monetary Fund. (2024, October 31). *Regional Economic Outlook for the Middle East and Central Asia, October 2024: Navigating the Evolving Geoeconomic Landscape.* International Monetary Fund. Available at https://www.imf.org/en/Publications/REO/MECA/Issues/2024/10/24/regional-economic-outlook-middle-east-central-asia-october-2024

Ismailov, E., & Papava, V. (2008). *The Central Caucasus: Problems of geopolitical economy.* Nova Science Publishers.

Jaspers, K. (1994). *Sense and Purpose of History.* Moscow.

Jenkins, L., & Pezant, P. (2003). *Central Asia: Reassessment of the Regional Transport Sector Strategy.* Asian Development Bank.

Joshi, N. (2010). *Reconnecting India and Central Asia: Emerging security and economic dimensions.* Washington, D.C.

Katz, M. N. (2001). *Revolution: International dimensions.* CQ Press.

Kaushik, D. (1985). *India and Central Asia in Modern Times.* Satvahan.

Kavalski, E. (2010). *The new Central Asia: The regional impact of international actors.* Singapore: World Scientific Publishing.

Kavalski, E. (2024). Competitive institutionalized cooperation in Central Asia: The politics of regionalism. *Central Asian Survey, 43*(1), 1–19

Kazharov, R., Nurova, N., & Safranchuk, I. (2012). Energeticheskoye sotrudnichestvo v ramkakh ShOS. Moscow.

King, C., & Mervin, N. J. (1998). *Nations abroad: Diaspora politics and international relations in the former Soviet Union.* Westview Press.

Kissinger, H. (1994). Diplomacy. Simon & Schuster.

Koldunova, E. (2010). Bezopasnost v Vostochnoi Azii: Novye vyzovy. Navona.

Korzhubaev, A. (2007). Forecast of the Development of the Oil and Gas Industry in Russia and Prospects for Forming New Energy Resource Export Routes. *Far Eastern Affairs*, 3, 35-46.

Kryukov, N. A. (2006). Evolution of Russian-Ukrainian Relations: The Legal Status of the Black Sea Fleet. *Military Thought*, 1, 1-8.

Kundu, D. N. (2006). Russia-Ukraine Gas Dispute. IDSA Strategic Comment, 13 January 2006

Kundu, D. N. (2012). 12th SCO Summit in Beijing: A view from India. *Valdai Discussion Club*. Retrieved from http://valdaiclub.com/asia/44660.html

Lailuma, N. (2015, October 11). Extremist movements in north a threat to Central Asia, experts. *The Kabul Times*. Available at http://thekabultimes. gov.af/index.php/opinions/politics/8335-extremist-movements-in-north-a-threat-to-central-asia-experts.html

Laruelle, M., & Peyrouse, S. (2012). *The Chinese question in Central Asia: Domestic order, social change, and the Chinese factor*. Hurst & Company.

Lin, G., Garver, J., Hickey, D., & Chambers, M. (2005). China's "good neighbor" diplomacy: A wolf in sheep's clothing? *Asia Program Special Report*, 126.

Lukin, A. (Ed.). (2012). Strategiya Rossii v Tsentralnoi Azii i Shankhayskoi organizatsii sotrudnichestva. MGIMO.

Lynch, D. (2000). *Russian Peacekeeping Strategies in the CIS: The Cases of Moldova, Georgia, and Tajikistan*. St. Martins Press.

Makovsky, A., & Sayarı, S. (2000). Changing dynamics of Turkish foreign policy. Washington Institute for Near East Policy.

Malcolm, N. (1996). *Internal Factors in Russian Foreign Policy*. Oxford University Press.

Malgin, A. (2002). *The Commonwealth of Independent States: Russian Politics and Law*, 40(5), 47-56.

Malik, H. Y. (2012). Strategic importance of Gwadar Port. *Journal of Political Studies*, 19, February.

Menon, R. (1998). After Empire: Russia and the Southern 'Near Abroad'. In M. Mandelbaum (Ed.), *The New Russian Foreign Policy* (pp. 100-166). Council on Foreign Relations Press.

Nakamur, Y. (1999). Extractive Industries and "Dutch Disease". Discussion Paper, 99/5, Department of Economics, Heriot-Watt University.

Nargis, K. (2014). Relations between Afghanistan and Central Asian states after 2014: Incentives, constraints, and prospects. *SIPRI*. Available at http://books.sipri.org/files/misc/SIPRI14wcaNK.pdf

Nuriyev, E. (2007). *South Caucasus at the Crossroads: Conflict, Caspian Oil, and Great Power Politics*. Li, Berlin.

Nygren, B. (2005). Russia's Relations with Ukraine and Belarus. In R. Kanet (Ed.), The New Security Environment: The Impact on Russia, Central and Eastern Europe (pp. 156-161). Ashgate.

Oliker, O. (2003). *Faultlines of Conflict in Central Asia and the South Caucasus*. RAND Corporation.

Omelicheva, M. Y. (2014). *Nationalism and identity construction in Central Asia: Dimensions, dynamics, and directions*. Lexington Books.

Parkash, M. (2006). *Connecting Central Asia: A road map for regional cooperation*. ADB Manila.

Patnaik, A. (2004). Russian Minorities in Central Asia. *World Focus*, 25(3), 13-15.

Phillips, A., & James, P. (2001). National identity between tradition and reflexive modernization: The contradictions of Central Asia. *National Identities*, 3(1).

Pincus, W. (2010, October 24). Bethesda-based development firm gets Kyrgyzstan contract. *Washington Post*.

Polanchek, S. (1980). Conflict and Trade. *Journal of Conflict Resolution*, 24(1), 55-78.

Pomfret, R. (2010). Trade and Transport in Central Asia. Emerging Markets Forum. *Centennial Group Report*.

Porter, B. D., & Saivetz, C. R. (1994). The Once and Future Empire: Russia and the 'Near Abroad'. *Washington Quarterly*, Summer, 17(3), 75-90.

Prevas, J. (2004). *Envy of the Gods: Alexander the Great's Ill-Fated Journey Across Asia*. De Capo Press.

Raballand, G., & Ferhat, E. (2007). Economics and Politics of Cross Border Oil Pipelines. *Asia Europe Journal*, 5(1), 133-146.

Rahimov, M. (2007). From Soviet republics to independent countries: Challenges of transition in Central Asia. *Perspectives on Global Development and Technology*, 6(1-3).

Rahimov, M., & Urazaeva, G. (2005). Central Asian nations and border issues. Conflict Studies Research Centre Report, *Central Asian Series*, 05/10, March.

Richard, F. (2010). *Religions of the Silk Road*. Palgrave Macmillan.

Rivera, D. W. (2003). Engagement, containment, and the international politics of Eurasia. *Political Science Quarterly*, 118(1), 81-104.

Rubinstein, A. Z. (1997). Russia: In Search of a New Role—Changing Geopolitical Compulsions in Central Asia. *World Affairs*, 1(2), 73-74.

Saidazimova, G. (2005, July 7). Kyrgyzstan: Youth playing key role in pro-Bakiyev political movement. RFE/RL. Saray, M. (1982). The Russian conquest of Central Asia. *Central Asian Survey*, 2(3).

Security Council Report. (2025, January 30). *UNRCCA (Central Asia), February 2025 Monthly Forecast*. Security Council Report. Retrieved from https://www.securitycouncilreport.org/monthly-forecast/2025-02/unrcca-central-asia-13.php

Simonsen, S. G. (2005). Between minority rights and civil liberties: Russia's discourse over 'nationality' registration and the internal passport. Nationalities Papers, 33(2), June.

Sims, M. (2005). Harmonization and Simplification of Transport Agreements, Cross-Border Documents and Transport Regulations. Report prepared for the Asian Development Bank.

Starr, F. (2005). A "Greater Central Asia Partnership" for Afghanistan and its neighbors. Silk Road Paper. Available athttp://www.silkroadstudies.org/ resources/pdf/SilkRoadPapers/2005_starr_a-greater-central-asia-partnership.pdf.

Starr, F. (2007). *The new Silk Road: Transport and trade in greater Central Asia*. John Hopkins University-SAIS.

Starr, F. (2016). The new Central Asia. *YouTube*. Available at https://www.youtube.com/watch?v=tIde2QSDwZk

Stulberg, A. (2005). Moving Beyond the Great Game. *Geopolitics*, 10(1), 1-25

Suleymanlı, A. (2009). The Baku-Tbilisi-Kars Railway Connection as an Important Section of the Trans-European Railway Network. Workshop on Rail Transport Between Europe and Asia, June 9-10, Istanbul.

Suny, R. (1991). Incomplete Revolution: National Movement and the Collapse of the Soviet Empire. *New Left Review*, 189, 111-125.

Tapiola, O. S. (2012). The Eurasian Customs Union: Friend or foe of the EU? Carnegie Papers, Carnegie Endowment for International Peace, Brussels, October.

Tarasyuk, B. (2004). A Ukrainian View of a New Euro-Atlantic Strategy in the Black Sea Area. The German Marshall Fund of the United States, 35-39.

Tishkov, V. A. (1995). The Russians in Central Asia and Kazakhstan. In Y. Ro'i (Ed.), Muslim Eurasia: Conflicting Legacies (pp. 292-295).

UN. (2003). Transit transport issues in landlocked and transit developing countries. Report No. ST/ESCAP/2270.

UN. (2013). International human development indicators. Retrieved from http://hdrstats.undp.org/en/indicators/103106.html

UNDP. (2004). Human Development Report, 2004: Cultural Library in Today's Diverse World. United Nations.

UNHCR. (2000). Central Asia regional overview. Global Report 2000. Available at http://www.unhcr.org/cgibin/texis/vtx/home/opendocPDF Viewer.html?docid=3e23eb617&query=afghans.

United Nations Economic and Social Commission for Asia and the Pacific. (2003). Transit Transport Issues in Landlocked and Transit Developing Countries. Report No. ST/ESCAP/2270.

Usher, A.P. (1930). The history of population and settlement in Eurasia. *Geographical Review*, 20(1), 30-45.

Vinokurov, E., Jadraliyev, M., & Shcherbanin, Y. (2009). The EurAsEC transport corridors: Sector report. Eurasian Development Bank.

Walt, S.M. (1991). The Renaissance of Security Studies. *International Studies Quarterly*, 35(2), 211-239.

Waugh, D. (2007). Richthofen's "Silk Roads": Toward the Archaeology of a Concept. *The Silk Road*, 5(1), 4.

Webber, M. (1996). *The International Politics of Russia and the Successor States*. Manchester University Press.

Weitz, R. (2009, February 10). Global security watch Russia: A reference handbook. *World Politics Review*.

Wilfred, J. E. (1998). Regionalism in a Multilateral World. *Journal of Political Economy*, 106(6), 1214-1245.

Wink, A. (2002). *Al-Hind: The Making of the Indo-Islamic World*. Brill Academic Publishers.

World Bank. (2005). Trade and Transport Facilitation in Central Asia: Reducing the Economic Distance to Markets. Final Report.

World Bank. (2006). From disintegration to reintegration: Europe and Central Asia in international trade.

World Bank. (2024). *Europe and Central Asia Economic Update*. World Bank. Retrieved from https://www.worldbank.org/en/region/eca/publication/ europe-and-central-asia-economic-update

Zadeh, P. M. (1999). The Geopolitics of the Caspian Region. In H. Amirahmadi (Ed.), The Caspian Region at the Crossroad: Challenges of New Frontiers of Energy and Development (pp. 175-179). St. Martin's Press.

Zbigniew, B. (1997). A geostrategy for Eurasia. *Foreign Affairs*, 76(5), 50-64.

Zharmagambetova, Z., & Flake, L. (2012). Kazakhstan: Grain and feed update. USDA Foreign Agricultural Service Global Agricultural Information Network (GAIN) Report.

Ziyadov, T. (2012). Azerbaijan as a Regional Hub in Central Eurasia. Azerbaijan Diplomatic Academy.

Index